Value-Added Leadership:
How to Get Extraordinary Performance in Schools

Thomas J. Sergiovanni
Trinity University

Value-Added Leadership:

How to Get

Extraordinary

Performance

in Schools

HBJ

Harcourt Brace Jovanovich, Publishers

HBJ Leadership

San Diego   New York   Chicago   Austin   Washington, D.C.

London   Sydney   Tokyo   Totonto

ISBN: 0-15-594702-8
Library of Congress Catalog Card Number: 89-84233
Printed in the United States of America

Foreword

What can be done to improve America's schools? While some agree that improvements are necessary, differences arise concerning what should be done. Yet beneath the disagreements, there is consensus on a fundamental premise: nothing will happen without leadership. From someone—or someplace—energy needs to be created, released, channeled, or mobilized to get the ball rolling in the right direction. Here again, however, there are multiple ideas about what leadership means or how it should be exercised. Some emphasize leadership as a humanistic enterprise—meeting peoples' needs and improving their skills motivates them to higher levels of performance. Others argue that leadership is more a matter of making sound decisions, creating sensible policies, and allocating rewards or penalities based on formal assessments of individual contributions to organizational goals. Still others see leadership as mostly political. Mobilizing power, building coalitions, and negotiating agreements among conflicting interest groups becomes the primary route through which leadership makes a difference. If one examines the recent slate of educational reforms, these three approaches to leadership are easily visible. For the most part, we seek to improve schools through retraining, restructuring, or empowering.

In the wings, however, another view of leadership awaits an entrance (or re-entrance). This perspective sees leadership as a more ephemeral, elusive force. It burrows beneath the surface of organizations—individuals, structure, or power—in search of symbolic forms and primordial archetypes. It accepts the mystical and expressive side of leadership and the possibility that organizations are governed as much by belief and faith as by rationality and outcome. Rather than improving organizations through motivation, reason, or negotiation, this approach emphasizes the restoration of spirit and heart. In this conception, leadership strikes a chord in followership that unites both in a meaningful enterprise, a beloved institution.

Sergiovanni's value-added leadership articulates one form of this deeper conception. It is brought to us by an academic who had the conviction to question earlier formulations of leadership in the light of his direct experiences with schools. Rather than to blame schools for their failure to conform to his theories, he revised his ideas to conform to the realities and possibilities of schools.

His approach is rooted mainly in the social science and business literatures. He suggests that the crucial task of improving schools is to rekindle gambare—in my words, spirit and heart. He argues that this will happen only through the influence of leaders who have beliefs, values, courage, and persistence. He reintroduces the idea of moral authority, a mantle conceived by Max Weber and won by the likes of Mr. Chips. It restores a form of authority somehow eclipsed by more modern views based on expertise, hierarchy, or legality. Sergiovanni reminds us of the importance of symbolic leadership, reviving ideas that Barnard, Selznick, and Arnold introduced decades ago. Somehow their ideas also succumbed to the modern assumption that technical/rational forms of leadership would yield greater dividends.

Sergiovanni's notion of value-added leadership is not a prescription. His central tenant, corollaries, and stages provide a framework for thinking about ways in which leaders can nourish the spirit of schools. His approach does not ignore the importance of power, structure, or motivation. But he sees the moral or spiritual revitalization of schools as a means of empowering, improving performance, or encouraging administrators or teachers to invest more energy in what they do. Undoubtedly there will be other forms of creative ideas that are waiting to make their entrance on the stage of school improvement and reform. But Sergiovanni has obviously provided us with a solid debut performance.

We are at a critical junction in our efforts to help schools improve. The problems are becoming more and more acute. And our remedies are becoming more and more important. But schools have built an immunity to strategies that are merely warmed-over versions of those that have failed in the recent past. Into what many have portrayed as a crisis, we need to interject possibilities that represent a break from recent memory and a return to historical fundamentals. Business has already realized that shared values and beliefs are essential to superior performance. A singular focus on the quarterly figures or the yearly bottom line breeds short-term strategies, often harmful to long-term success. Federal Express, for example, operates on one simple premise: "people, service, profits . . . in that order." The company is in business to make money. But executives and employees believe that profit is a derivation of an emphasis on people and service. Values, not profits drive most successful businesses in the United States.

In the wake of Vietnam, military organizations have also come to the realization that successful performance is more than a matter of numbers and technology. In the words of Admiral Carlisle Trest, Chief of Naval Operations, "it is people, not systems that deter and win wars." He goes on to argue "that leadership is flesh and blood," not a sterile anticipation exercise of command decision. The U.S. Air Force has added another dimension to Clausewitz's original fundamentals: "cohesion is a principle of war." Like businesses, military organizations have realized that you rarely manage people into difficult circumstances, you lead them.

In a sense, U.S. schools are currently locked in a war against ignorance and apathy. Whether we win or lose will depend, in large part, on leadership that can restore a moral fiber to classrooms and schools. It seems highly improbable that much significant improvement will happen if teachers continue to think of themselves as "just teachers," or if administrators persevere in the assumption that clearer goals or more rigorous evaluation will solve the problems. What is needed instead is a return to or revision of values and beliefs that resanctify the business of education. Some McDonald's franchises show more enthusiasm for hamburger buns than educators demonstrate in working with young people. Now is the time to recommit ourselves to the sacred trust that is given to those who prepare the next generation for challenges that lie ahead. That will require a fundamental shift in the viewpoint of many educators. It will involve a rekindling of what it means to be a teacher. It most definitely implies rethinking and reshaping our leadership premises and practices. As I read Sergiovanni's manuscript, I imagined what I would do next if I were in a formal or informal position of leadership in a public school.

My first step would be to revisit my decision to enter the profession. If I could not remember a passionate, principled rationale for my choice, I would resign or retire and do something else. I know I could probably make more money with fewer headaches and less heartburn.

Assuming that I could recall a "fire in the belly" that called me to education because of a sense that I could make a difference, I would write down some heartfelt principles, values, and beliefs. They would center around what I believe to be good for children and young people—now and in the future. What do I stand for? What, of value, do I want to contribute to young people or society?

I would then search internally to see whether or not I had the courage to take the heat that might be generated by acting on these beliefs. If I wasn't willing to "go to jail" to uphold these values or beliefs (as reporters do to protect a source) then I would think about retirement, a safer field, or a cushy management position in a district planning and evaluation operation.

But if I felt passionate about my values and positive about my fortitude, I would accept Sergiovanni's challenge. I would accept the challenge of leadership and the extraordinary investment it would require. I would think about mission and symbols and how I could encourage others to join me in a meaningful quest. I would give people opportunities and hold them and myself accountable for attaining shared outcomes. I would do anything possible to create a community of colleagues. I would be willing to be outrageous in demonstrating my commitments, deceptive in fending off unneeded bureaucratic trappings, and moral in doing the right things rather than doing things right.

Once I got my act together, I would use Sergiovanni's framework to engage a school (or district) in the process of improvement—pushing, supporting, inspiring, or monitoring as necessary as the collective that is worked through the stages. I would see myself as a participant in a communal tai-chee tournament to exchange energy in pursuit of an organization we would all ultimately be proud of.

During all this, I would remind myself of the power of human organization to resist improvement, to resent leadership, and to remain in a comfortable status quo—even one that's not working very well. From time to time, I might reread Sergiovanni's book. And I suspect that I would be constantly nourished by the maxim—"the worse the screw-up, the better the story." Adding value to the human experience is not always easy. But if you want to leave a mark, you have to take some risks. The people who have are those we remember—Jesus Christ, Martin Luther King, Joan of Arc, or Ghandi. We need more leadership like theirs to improve America's schools. In Sergiovanni's words, we need more value-added rather than value-neutral leadership in education.

Terrence E. Deal
Vanderbilt University
Co-author of
Corporate Cultures

Preface

My intention in writing this book is to provide a clear, compelling, and practical view of leadership for both educational professionals and those within the general public who are interested not only in improving schools but in helping them achieve extraordinary results. I propose value-added leadership as the means to get this job done. This proposal recognizes that leadership is only part of the equation for quality schooling. Needed, too, is concern for first-rate teaching, sound curriculum, sensible evaluation practices, parental involvement, issues of equity, and political and financial support. But none of these concerns can be fully attended to in the absence of the right leadership.

Starting with the value of traditional leadership, value-added leadership adds the ingredients needed to inspire extraordinary performance. To achieve this goal I decided to forgo the usual scholarly trappings that typically characterize books in the social and management sciences and to adopt instead a more straightforward approach. In 1892, the eminent philosopher–psychologist William James was asked by Harvard University to give a series of lectures for teachers of the town of Cambridge. The lectures were subsequently published in a book entitled *Talks to Teachers on Psychology: And to Students on Some of Life's Ideals* published by Henry Holt and Company. I take comfort from the comments James wrote in the preface of his book:

> I have found by experience that what my hearers seem least to relish
> is analytical technicality, and what they most care for is concrete
> practical application. So I have gradually weeded out the former and

left the latter unreduced; and now that I have at least written out the lectures, they contain a minimum of what is themed 'scientific' in psychology and are practical and popular in the extreme.

Some of my colleagues may possibly shake their heads at this; but in taking my cue from what has seemed to me to be the feeling of the audiences I believe that I am shaping my book so as to satisfy the more genuine public need.

I want to thank all of the supervisors, principals, and superintendents who participated in my study of memorable, leadership-critical incidents. The list of participants is too long to provide. Unless otherwise noted in the references, the "stories" used to illustrate value-added leadership concepts are from this study. The incidents from the study not retold in the book were nonetheless important in helping me to understand the "stuff" of value-added leadership. I have also included stories, incidents, and examples that were accumulated as part of the research of a score of others. The concept of value-added leadership, therefore, emerges from a decade or so of research and reflections by many people. Further, its basic components and characteristics have been individually known to successful leaders throughout recorded history. As Alfred North Whitehead reminds us, "Everything of importance has been said before by someone who did not invent it." *Value Added Leadership* brings together these individual insights into a new and powerful model of school leadership practice.

Anyone casually acquainted with the emerging literature on leadership will recognize my debt to the writings of such individuals as Anthony G. Athos, Bruce G. Barnett, Bernard Bass, Peter Block, Lee G. Bolman, John Champlin, David C. Dwyer, William Firestone, John W. Gardner, John Goodlad, William Greenfield, Gene Hall, Philip Hallinger, Shirley Hord, Ann Lieberman, Alan Kennedy, James M. Kouzes, Ginny V. Lee, Sara L. Lightfoot, James G. March, John Meyer, Lawrence M. Miller, Lynne Miller, Joseph Murphy, William Ouchi, Robert Owens, Richard Tanner Pascale, Thomas J. Peters, Louis Pondy, Barry Z. Posner, Robert E. Quinn, Edgar Schein, Robert H. Waterman, and Bruce Wilson. I owe a special debt to Warren Bennis of the University of Southern California; Terence E. Deal of Vanderbilt University; Judith Little of the Far West Lab; Roland Barth of Harvard

University; Jane Ann Kendrick, principal of the Eggars Middle School in Hammond, Indiana; Joan Lipsitz of the Lilly Foundation; Judy Lechner Knowles, principal of the George Washington Elementary School in Philadelphia; Janet Mort, superintendent of the Saanichton Schools in British Columbia; Philip Schlechty of the Jefferson County, Kentucky, schools; Karl Weick of the University of Michigan, Marshal Sashkin of the U.S. Department of Education, and Robert J. Starratt of Fordham University. Their work was particularly important in helping me to develop the concept of value-added leadership. James MacGregor Burn's work on transactional and transformative leadership was seminal.

I thank my students taught during 19 years at the University of Illinois in Urbana-Champaign, who almost without exception now rank among the best of the best when it comes to school leaders, and my students at Trinity University, who helped me to understand better the links between value-added leadership and the expansive nature of human potential.

And finally, I am grateful to the hundreds of school leaders throughout the United States, Canada, Australia, and New Zealand with whom I have been privileged to work. It is, after all, a lot easier to write a book on leadership than to provide it. All I had to do was tell their story. *Value-Added Leadership: How to Get Extraordinary Performance in Schools* is, therefore a tribute to them and a celebration of their success.

Thomas J. Sergiovanni

Contents

Gambare! Getting Extraordinary Performance in Schools

Gambare *means "to persevere; to do one's best; to be persistent; to stick to one's purposes; to never give up until the job is done and done well."*

America's schools can work well. Enough examples of excellence exist to prove that point. Indeed our best schools compare favorably with the best schools of other countries; but it is no secret that too many of our schools are not functioning as well as they should. It is estimated that roughly three-quarters of a million students who graduate from our high schools are functionally illiterate. Another three-quarters of a million students drop out. Among blacks and Hispanics the dropout rate hovers at around 50 percent. Too many teachers are dissatisfied, teacher performance and commitment is uneven, parental disinterest is high, and students are frequently disengaged from the school having displaced school purposes with those of their own. Despite important exceptions the process of schooling has become routine, even boring and mechanistic. Too often the zip and excitement seem to be gone for both teachers and students. A certain malaise, disconnectedness, and defensiveness characterize the system. Confusion exists over what needs to be done. A common purpose seems to be lacking. Yes, some schools are getting the job done and done well but too many are not.

School, for too many students who stay, is a place to be rather than a place to become.

Present efforts to fix the schools have achieved mixed results. Too many of the proposed remedies have become part of the problem resulting in stifling overregulation, increased bureaucracy and wasteful inefficiency. Standardization, the great ally of mediocrity, wins out too often over imagination. The result is a stagnated system of schooling incapable of providing for America's social and economic needs in an age of increased global competition.

What happens in schools is in part influenced by and a reflection of larger trends in our society. America's institutions are interdependent in complex ways. As one goes, so go the rest. Thus, it comes as no surprise to find that when corporate America shines, the schools also shine and vice versa. Declining market shares, unfavorable production and efficiency comparisons with our international competition, sinking quality, poor customer service, and deteriorating worker commitment in corporate America have paralleled declines in schooling. When one examines economic statistics and student achievement statistics side by side it becomes clear that we have been outfoxed by the competition in both the corporate boardroom and the schoolroom.

Corporate America has begun to bounce back. Chief executive officer of the Xerox Corporation, David T. Kearns, points out, "American business fell behind, not just because the Japanese were better, but because we were committed to ossified management structures. It wasn't just that our plant and equipment needed replacing. Our entire way of thinking needed to be replaced. Not just updated or revamped—replaced!"[1] Kearns points out that today's successful companies bear little resemblance to those of ten to twenty years ago. They are flatter in structure and more decentralized in decision making relying on the knowledge and professionalism of workers who deal with problems on a daily basis."

By contrast, Kearns points out that too many American schools and school systems still hang on to the very archaic, outmoded, and discredited management practices that have been abandoned in corporate America. In his words, most of our large school districts "are organized like a factory of the late 19th century: top down, command-control management, a system designed to stifle creativity and independent judgment."[2] San Diego City Schools Superintendent Thomas W. Payzant puts it this way: "Most schools in America are structured today much like the schools that existed at the turn of the century. Functioning as modern factories, they select, sort, grade, and process students. . . . There is an assembly-line process that propels those who participate through a maze that successfully negotiated leads to annual promotion and ultimately a high school diploma. Too many fall off the assembly line. We call them dropouts."[3]

It is now time for our schools to recover. But this recovery will not occur unless America's school establishment—from the governor's office to the superintendent's office, from the state agency to the class-room—begins to understand what is now being understood in both the private sector *and* in many successful schools. We have for too long hung on to an inadequate theory of management and a leadership practice that is incapable of turning around failing situations on the one hand and of turning ordinary situations into extraordinary ones on the other. Relying on this theory as the basis for developing school-improvement policies and for practicing leadership promises at worst further decay and at best continued stagnation. The consequences for social and economic America are grave.

Despite the problems, there are enough examples of successful schools to make this a hopeful time. The challenge we face is to make the exception the rule. When one examines leadership in successful schools one finds a unique kind and quality of leadership and a different perspective on the part of leaders than that found elsewhere. These leaders practice value-added leadership. I will draw upon the practices of successful leaders to provide an analysis of how this new leadership works and suggestions for how this new leadership might come to dominate our educational system.

Value-added leadership builds upon sound management ideas that have served us well in the past. It is clear as we approach the twenty-first century, that sound management, applied in moderation, needs to be viewed as a necessary but *insufficient* ingredient in thinking about school-improvement strategies and school practice. The answer I propose and describe in this book is to "add value" to that which we have.

Value-added leadership emerges from a synthesis of traditional management and social science and recent studies of successful school and corporate cultures. Both old and new (value and value-added) theories of leadership are brought together into a powerful model of practice that seeks first to secure a satisfactory level of performance and commitment from teachers and students, and then to achieve extraordinary performance.

School administrators practice value leadership when they seek a fair return to the school from teachers and students for its investments in them. Investments are in the form of financial, psychological, social and educational benefits that the school provides. The returns sought from teachers and students are the time and effort needed to make the school work the way it should. "A fair day's work" is asked for "a fair day's pay." Value leadership can successfully manage this exchange by providing the direction, resources, facilitating conditions, incentives, and supervision that are necessary to clarify, support, and reward what needs to be done. Value is achieved when school and participants each get what they bargained for—school expectations are met and participants are fairly rewarded. Breakdowns can occur in value leadership when teachers and students are not sure what they must do to get what they want, when no system of support is provided that helps them to meet school expectations, when wants are misunderstood, and when an effective system for monitoring and adjusting this exchange is not in place. The breakdown of value leadership in a school threatens its ability to function at an acceptable level. Over time the inevitable result is incompetent management and inadequate schooling!

It is true that many schools and school districts would benefit enormously if school leaders would only practice competent value leadership. In some schools the problem is not that school leaders are incapable of practicing value leadership but that they are unable to engage in such practice. This is the case in many larger school districts where excessive bureaucracy reigns and in some states where excessive regulations have resulted in legislated learning and bureaucratic teaching. America's main problem, however, is not bad but mediocre schools. Only value-added leadership can raise our schools from the malaise of mediocrity to excellence. Excellence must become the norm if we seek the economic prosperity needed to care for our people, our culture, and our institutions with grace, comfort, and security in the twenty-first century. At stake here is not a theory of leadership or a point of view on schooling but the nature of the human condition and the quality of life that will characterize our nation's future. Thus the word *added* is critical. When value and value-added leadership are practiced together value-added provides the bridge between helping teachers and students meet basic expectations and achieving levels of performance and commitment that are extraordinary.

Value-added leadership can help to restore the spirit of "Gambare!" in our schools and in society itself. The process of schooling in America is often characterized by complacency with respect to effort and self-centeredness with respect to goals—a condition that too frequently characterizes American life itself. Christopher Lasch hauntingly described this problem in his widely read book *The Culture of Narcissism American Life in an Age of Diminishing Expectations.*[4] Too often deals are struck in America's classrooms whereby students trade with teachers minimally accepted behavior for minimal academic demands. You don't hassle me with having to learn too much and I won't hassle you by being a discipline problem or by skipping school. Under these conditions academic content and work demands are displaced by conversational teaching or "nonteaching" in an effort to ensure good student relationships and classroom order or to just ensure that students show up. Since school funding formulas are based on the number of students who attend each day, getting kids to come to school even if they are not taught or don't learn is a major school priority.

In investigating the nature of such deals in several high schools Michigan State University researcher Phillip Cusick notes, "The basic requirement for teachers was not that they instruct from some agreed-upon course of study. It was not even that they instructed. It was that they be capable of maintaining some state of moderate order among the students and the proof that they could do this was that their students were neither running about the halls nor showing up in the office. One could instruct, one could not instruct; it was up to the individual teacher to decide how to conduct himself or herself in the classroom. The requirement at all the schools was that he or she be able to maintain order among the students."[5] One of the teachers in Cusick's study put it this way:

> This girl missed 55 days of classes, 55 days and she hadn't handed in an assignment since I checked my book since October 10 and so I flunked her from the class. But the parent came in and talked to the principal, so I got called in and he said, looking right at me, "Mr. -----, is it necessary to fail that student?" and I said, "Yes" and showed him what I'm showing you, and then he looked at me and said, "Is it really

necessary to fail that student?" I said, "Yes," but the third time he said it, I got the message.[6]

The trading of standards for behavior is a theme, as well, in Theodore Sizer's book *Horace's Compromise*. The agreement takes the form of a "facade of orderly purposefulness"[7] under which teachers and students exchange minimums in pursuit of the least hassle for everyone.

More disheartening that this scaling down of commitment and performance is the displacement of teaching and learning as the goal and purpose of schooling in too many of our schools. The problem is particularly acute in our urban centers. Bureaucratic rules and regulations, administrative convenience, the provisions of the labor-management contract, and the interests and welfare of teachers take precedence over and sometimes replace the interests of students and the community. Forgotten in the selfish scramble for convenience and advantage are questions of why school decisions are made, for what purpose, and who benefits.

Let's put the question of who benefits from school decisions to a test. Develop a mental image of a grid similar to the one provided in Exhibit 1–1. Use the grid to record the prime beneficiaries of decisions that have been made recently in your school or another school with which you are familiar. At the top of your grid list several of the possible prime beneficiaries. Administrators, teachers, students, bureaucratic system, parents, industry, universities, and society are listed in the grid provided. To the left of the grid list a half-dozen or so decisions made recently in the school you are analyzing, checking off the prime beneficiaries for each.

Consider the following example. Chicago, New York City, and many other large districts have had extensive seniority provisions written into their union contracts. Such provisions frequently allow senior teachers to bump any junior teacher from an assignment that they covet. Such bumping often elicits a chain reaction resulting in several teachers being displaced. Principals have little or no control over who gets bumped into or out of their school, thus making the building of a stable school faculty difficult. When bumping is triggered by the elimination of positions held by senior teachers (as might happen in the case of declining enrollments in a particular school) the chain of events inevitably means job losses for less senior teachers, regardless

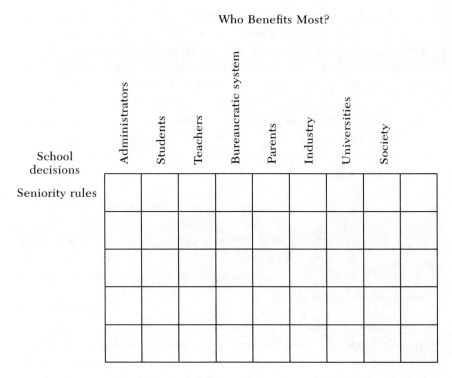

Exhibit. 1–1. The Prime Beneficiary Grid.

of their capability and record of performance. Furthermore, the most senior teachers typically wind up in the "best" schools with the "easiest" students to teach while beginning teachers are overrepresented in the most difficult teaching assignments. Instability from the seniority and licensing system can often result in students being taught by several different teachers in the same academic year. Who benefits from such practices? Certainly not students or parents.

Consider another example cited in *Education Week*. When Beth J. Fuqua reported for her first teaching assignment as a fourth-grader teacher in a Brooklyn elementary school (she received the assignment on a Thursday with school opening four days later) she had to scramble to get her classroom ready. On Friday she was able to get her supplies and class list but no books or curriculum guides were available. Indeed no books were available on Monday, the first day of class. When she asked her assistant principal about the books, *Education Week* reports his response as follows: "Well, about the books, you probably won't get them for two or three weeks, because the person in charge of the book room won't be in until then."[8] When asked for a key to the book room the assistant principal is reported as refusing noting that the principal didn't want anyone rummaging around in the book room getting things disorganized. Once again students and parents lose in the competition for being the prime beneficiary of school decisions. It is appropriate for teachers and administrators to be prime beneficiaries of many school decisions; but when the overwhelming number of such decisions consistently do not primarily benefit students and the community, America is in trouble.

The restoration of prominence in our school system will require that some of the spirit, drive, commitment, and sense of moral responsiveness that brought about such prominence in the first place be recaptured. Value-added leadership can help in this effort. It has the capacity to renew the American spirit and to set us back on the track to success once again.

We can learn a great deal about renewing our spirit from the Japanese, even though their *model* of schooling is not for us. The Japanese model is based on conformity. The curriculum is set by the national ministry of education; texts are standardized; and all schools have the same administrative structure, the same daily schedule, the same classroom and office arrangements, the same number of students, and even the same seating arrangement for students. This "machine" approach to education fits their culture but not ours. Peggy Lukens, an American high school English teacher who taught in Japanese high schools, explains: "Japanese education is designed from the top down to suit Japan's society—a society different from ours in significant ways. While democratic reforms may have arrived in Japan in 1945, it remains at its core a hierarchical, authoritarian, conservative, and largely homogeneous society."[9] Japanese schools have been very successful in producing uniformly competent standard products, but not in preparing inventive, problem-solving thinkers. Since the war, for example, Japan has had 6 Nobel prize winners and the United States has had 144.

Nonetheless, the fact is that too many of our schools perform below their levels, and we can learn a good deal from them. We need to get better by copying the *nonmodel* aspects of the Japanese system and

avoiding the *model* aspects—hierarchical structure, centralized curriculum, excessive testing programs, and direct teaching methods. The
nonmodel aspects include the important role parents play in supporting the school, the enthusiasm that parents have for accepting a
share of the responsibility for the education of their children, and the
pervasiveness of the value of *gambare* in the Japanese culture. Much
of their success in corporate and educational life can be attributed to
the spirit of gambare. *Gambare* means "to persevere; to do one's best;
to be persistent; to stick to one's purposes; to never give up until the
job is done and done well." Japanese children begin formal indoctri-
nation in the tradition of gambare on the very first day that they enter
kindergarten and this tradition remains a part of their personality for
life, carrying forth from school to the workplace, from leisure to work
activities. In all that is to be done one must gambare.[10]

Japanese children are taught informally and formally that Japan
is not a great nation, but rather a nation whose position in the world's
scheme of things is precarious. The underdog role is instilled early
in children and carries through to adult life. The health and welfare
of Japan rests not with natural resources or serendipity but with the
tenacity, willingness, and ability of its people to struggle, to sacrifice,
to work hard, in effect, to gambare. Gambare is the reincarnation of
the Protestant work ethic in modern Japan. How ironic that this very
quality which loomed large in America's early successes seems now
to be on the decline. To be sure in an absolute sense America is not
an underdog in education or commerce, but in a relative sense (for
example in the last 20 years) we are. Yet, instead of gambare Americans
seem more attracted to mottos that tell us we are number one. It is
time for the more somber Avis approach, "We try harder."

Overcoming complacency will not be easy. As Benjamin Duke
points out in his analysis of Japanese and American schools, the American social studies and history curriculum provides a view of the world
that overplays the superiority of American society. In his words, "The
illustrious contributions of the United States to the world in the modern era come bursting through the pages of our classroom texts. From
music to literature to political theories to industrial might, U.S. accomplishments have been taken for granted in our teachings as well
as in our various media, which greatly influences our youth's social
attitudes. A smug complacency of superiority is admittedly hard to

counter in our schools."[11] His remedy is to incorporate into our schools a seriousness of purpose that is similar to the Japanese tradition of gambare—perseverance. He points out that, when leaders get too far ahead of the pack, it becomes difficult for them to maintain the diligence necessary to preserve their advantage. He considers complacency to be the source of the decline and fall of earlier Western civilizations, and cautions that this same complacency is an ever-present danger in the United States today. Duke is right in his assessment that much can be done in schools to provide our students with a more accurate portrayal of our newly emerging world order. We are barely ahead, and if we are to stay ahead we simply must restore the spirit of gambare in our schools and in our culture itself.

Value-added leadership can help restore the value of gambare to America's schools and life itself. Leadership is a very powerful force that can deeply influence the drive and commitments of teachers and students much more than the use of authority and management controls. The latter typically engender *subordinate* feelings and behaviors. Subordinates always do what they are supposed to; but they respond with little passion and rarely go beyond, to extraordinary levels of commitment and performance. Leadership, on the other hand, relies on values and ideas and when properly understood and practiced engenders *followership* feelings and behaviors in teachers and students. Followers respond to beliefs and ideas rather than controls. They respond with passion and commitment and their performance is typically beyond that expected of subordinates.

The behavior of successful leaders is often driven by a deep commitment to ideas and ideals they believe to be important. They speak often of the importance of perseverence and persistence—to hold the course, to keep trying, to try again, and to try harder in pursuit of one's convictions. They communicate to others that good enough is okay for today but not good enough for tomorrow. They are constantly pushing themselves and others forward by their words, behavior, and deeds. As they speak and live gambare this value becomes instilled as part of the life of the school—touching teachers, students, and parents.

Leaders can instill the value of gambare in their schools and districts by modeling perseverance. In their study of events in the lives of executives that seemed key to success, Center for Creative Leadership researchers Esther H. Lindsey Virginia Homes, and Morgan W. McCall, Jr., were able to identify three forms of perseverance:

Standing up for one's beliefs even when personal risk is involved and despite opposition.

Moving ahead in seeking to accomplish one's goals despite obstacles and detours.

Surviving tough times by "hanging in," being patient and coming back strong after a lost battle, mistake, or other setback.[12]

Common to the three is the leader's commitment to a value, principle, or idea; belief in her or his ability to develop ways to accomplish her or his goal in face of obstacles; and recognition that difficult situations are often not out of one's control.

Let's examine gambare in the leadership practices of school administrators. Some principals respond to the heightened vandalism that characterizes many of our schools today by letting their buildings decay. They reason that fixing toilets and windows only invites more damage. To avoid damage doors are often removed from stalls, mirrors are removed from walls, and amenities such as soap and toilet paper are not provided. To protect books from being damaged by students library doors are chained and teaching materials are withheld. Green grass is replaced with gravel and cement, telephones and soft drink machines are hidden away in the principal's office and teachers' lounge (although some teachers may argue about that latter point). In cases such as these principals allow vandals and thieves to decide school policies and to determine the rules and conditions of life in the school for everyone. This is leadership by default, a condition that plagues too many schools.

Under leadership by default, persistence and perseverance give way to an ugly vision of schooling that communicates immediacy rather than growth, survival rather than standards, and despair rather than hope. The lowest common denominator of human existence charts the course for everyone in the school.

Successful principals are not likely to settle for this chain of events. Leadership by default is just not part of their vocabulary. Faced with similar conditions the principal of Los Angeles's Locke High School, for example, refused to yield to vandals. The plantings he installed around the school in huge flower pots were ripped out by students on 15 occasions and replaced by him on each of the 15 occasions. A cinder block wall near the school entrance was repaired every time ugly scribbles of graffiti appeared. As the principal practiced gambare several messages were clear. A clean and attractive building builds pride. Vandals don't run the school, the principal does. Despite the behavior of some students, other students deserve to live and learn in a clean and attractive school. We are committed to quality standards and if you want to fight us you can, but don't bet on winning. If we believe something is right and worth doing, then it is right and worth doing even though the going is tough. In the principal's words, "We're going to be successful. . . . We're going to break this cycle of despair. I believe that the future of this country starts right here in Watts."[13] In other words he was shouting gambare!

In a similar vein the noted educational consultant William W. Purkey tells the story of a principal in a crowded high school who placed a potted plant in the center of a busy school corridor in an effort to achieve some semblance of order during class changes. The potted plant was to serve as a "silent cop" by helping to route the flow of traffic. The plant was mangled by students within hours of its first appearance. It was replaced by another larger plant that quickly met the same fate. Undaunted, the principal continued to replace damaged plants with still larger ones until the message was clear to students as to who was in charge; and the desired traffic pattern was achieved.[14]

Persistence and perseverance on behalf of one's values and beliefs are qualities of leadership that transcend different situations. They apply, for example, in schools that are struggling to reach a satisfactory level of competence and in good schools that could be even better. Good may be good enough for today but not for tomorrow. This is the view of Greg Voelz, an elementary school principal in Loveland, Colorado.

When Voelz became principal he found a competent staff hard at work, but a staff that was inclined to be complacent about its presumed quality, rarely reflecting on what it was doing and why, and rarely striving to be better. When he tried to address this issue, the staff's attitude was as follows: "We are already the best school in the district. We aren't broken so don't try to fix us." Not satisfied with this response and unwilling to be guided by the well-known management adage "Let sleeping dogs lie," he reminded the faculty of the importance of humility as they evaluated themselves and cautioned them about "flying high" regarding their presumed accomplishments and standing. He acknowledged that without question they were good—very good! He made it clear, nonetheless, that part of being good was being committed to getting better. He then announced that for the upcoming year everyone's present grade level teaching assignment was up for grabs. Each person would have to win back his or her assignment by arguing compellingly for it. He asked each teacher to meet with him to explain why they should stay in the same assignment. As part of the interview each teacher was asked to reflect on her or his teaching by describing what they did and why; by coming to grips with teaching habits and routines they had taken for granted; and by acknowledging areas in which they would like to grow, as well as new directions they would like to pursue. Nearly all the teachers won back their assignments; but more importantly nearly all the teachers were touched by the process in a positive way. A dialogue was begun within the faculty about what each was up to and why, and a renewed commitment to greater openness and improvement evolved. It is more difficult for a principal to focus the attention of a highly competent and successful faculty on self-reflection and improvement than it is with a lesser faculty. It can be done, however, if one brings to his or her practice determination and persistence on behalf of values and ideals.

Our young are not only a precious resource but a scarce resource. Harold L. Hodgkinson points out, that during our lifetime we will have more Americans over 65 than teenagers. "For the next fifteen years at least, we will have to work harder with the limited number of young people we have to work with. ... The task will be not to lower the standards but to increase the effort."[15] Gambare is key to getting extraordinary performance in schools. Without the will and determination to do better—to be better—not much will happen as a result of efforts to improve our schools. In the next chapter let's turn to the basic dimensions and characteristics of value-added leadership that can help us transform will and effort into reality.

2

Value-Added Leadership:

The Nine Dimensions and Two Corollaries that Lead to Extraordinary Performance

The principles of value-added leadership are as simple as they are powerful. They represent a set of ideas that have withstood the test of time despite the coming and going of leadership fads and the evolutionary progression of scholarly advances in psychological and managerial leadership technology. Sometimes the principles sound a bit like "motherhood and apple pie" causing many to conclude that they are too virtuous to be taken seriously. For some they are difficult to talk and write about; therefore, their appearance in general management literature and in curricula of schools of education and business administration has been slow. Recent studies of successful schools and corporations, however, have begun to change this picture. These studies show that successful leaders not only understand value-added principles, but that they practice them with a vengeance.[1]

In this chapter a basic framework for value-added leadership is provided. The framework comprises nine value-added dimensions with corresponding value dimensions and two corollaries. Though successful school leaders know the importance of value-added dimensions often the audiences they serve (school boards, state bureaucrats, politicians, and so on) do not, demanding instead exclusive attention to value dimensions. Successful school leaders handle this problem by saying and doing some things to get the legitimacy and freedom they need which then enables them to say and do other things that count toward quality schooling. The two corollaries are provided to help understand this seemingly contradictory slice of organizational reality. The remaining chapters in this book describe in fuller detail these dimensions and corollaries and provide examples of how they are lived and practiced by successful school leaders. The basic framework for value-added leadership is outlined below:

A. **Value Dimensions**
The emphasis is on:

Value-Added Dimensions
The emphasis is on:

	Value Dimensions	Value-Added Dimensions
1.	Management	Leadership
2.	Participation investment	Extraordinary performance investment
3.	Manipulating situations	Providing symbols and enhancing meaning
4.	Planning	Purposing
5.	Giving directions	Enabling teachers and the school
6.	Providing a monitoring system	Building an accountability system
7.	Extrinsic motivation	Intrinsic motivation
8.	Congeniality	Collegiality
9.	Calculated leadership	Leadership by outrage

B. **The Four Stages of Leadership for School Improvement**

	Stage:	*Leadership by:*	*Dimension:*
1.	Initiation (getting started)	Bartering (push)	Value
2.	Uncertainty (muddling through)	Building (support)	Value-added
3.	Transformative (breakthrough)	Bonding (inspire)	Value-added
4.	Routinization (remote control)	Banking (monitor)	Value-added

---

C. **The Two Corollaries**
   1. Build in Canvas

   2. Emphasize Moral Leadership

Key to the concept of value-added leadership is understanding that ordinarily one should not have to choose between value and value-added. Both dimensions of leadership are needed if schools are to measure up to minimum standards and also to reach out to achieve a level of performance and success that is beyond expectations—indeed extraordinary. The value dimensions determine the competence side of the ledger. Their presence ensures that schools will function in a competent manner. The inevitable consequence of their absence is incompetence. But competence and excellence are not the same. School excellence cannot be achieved by refining or increasing emphasis on the value dimensions of leadership. Excellence requires that the emphasis shift from value to value-added dimensions, and these are cut from a different bolt of cloth.

When shifting the emphasis from value to value-added, sometimes the trick is to build added value to that which already exists. This is the strategy suggested in the four stages of leadership for school improvement. (The four stages will be discussed further and illustrated in chapter 3.) At other times the initial value dimensions need to be transcended. A good accountability system, for example, is not just built upon the process of monitoring but literally transcends the process, making monitoring a needed managerial tool but not the foundation or substance of accountability. To keep things simple "emphasizing the value-added dimensions" will be used to suggest either a shift in emphasis from one dimension to the other or the transcending of one over the other as appropriate.

Emphasizing Leadership

Few would argue that schools can work well without the presence of competent management, but too often school officials at both state and local levels provide little else. Consequently too many schools, school districts and state systems of schooling are overmanaged and underled. This condition leads to an undue emphasis on doing things right rather than doing the right things; on following directions rather than solving problems. In searching for the proper balance between management and leadership H. Ross Perot, the founder of Electronic Data Systems Corporation, puts it this way: "Our country needs strong effective leaders willing to sacrifice to make this country strong. We need to stop managing and start leading."[2] Perot operates on the basis of a very simple principle: "People cannot be managed. Inventories can be managed, but people must be led."[3] Bob Ansett, president of Budget Rent-a-Car, Australia, states: "I probably place more emphasis on Leadership than most company managers, and I do that because I really believe that it is the only way you can establish the right sort of spirit, the commitment that you require, the commitment that is required by a team of people to achieve, and the emphasis on achievement is very high in my organization."[4]

Prior to beginning the research for their landmark book, *In Search of Excellence: Lessons from America's Best-Run Companies,* Thomas J. Peters and Robert H. Waterman, Jr. questioned the importance of leadership. "We must admit that our bias at the beginning was to discount the role of leadership heavily if for no other reason than that everybody's answer to what's 'wrong' or 'right' with whatever organization is its leader. Our strong belief was that the excellent companies had gotten to be the way they were because of a unique set of cultural attributes that distinguish them from the rest, and if we understand those attributes well enough, we could do more than just mutter 'leadership' in response to questions like 'why is *J* and *J* so good?' Unfortunately, what we found was that associated with almost every excellent company was a strong leader (or two) who seemed to have had a lot to do with making the company excellent in the first place."[5]

Unfortunately, ingrained school bureaucracy and highly prescriptive state regulations often prevent principals and superintendents from exercising the leadership that is needed. This is why Xerox Corporation's CEO David T. Kearns believes that schools need to be reorganized in such a way that no one but the school superintendent be paid more than the school principal; that central office staff become staff to principals in a system of site-based management rather than another layer of management to which schools must report.[6] Extending his argument one could reason that state departments of education should be slimmed down similarly and that their responsibilities be changed from trying to run the schools from afar to that of setting standards, evaluating standards, and providing help to local schools where needed. This new state role would allow the superintendents, principals, and teachers to provide the needed leadership.

The views of corporate leaders are highlighted in this discussion to point out that the need for leadership to be emphasized over management is not a partisan issue put forth by a self-indulgent member of the educational establishment but a necessity if we aspire to quality schooling. Numerous studies of successful schools point to the same conclusion. No matter how competently managed a school may be, it is the extra quality of leadership that makes the difference between ordinary and extraordinary performance.

Emphasizing the Performance Investment

A basic principle in work motivation theory and practice is that people invest in work to obtain desired returns or rewards. What is not understood by many who seek to improve our schools is that two very different investments are at stake, each linked to a very different set of returns and rewards—the participation investment and the performance investment. When teachers and principals make the participation investment they meet minimum contractual requirements—they give a fair day's work for a fair day's pay. This is the traditional legal work relationship between employer and employee. Unfortunately for those who settle for this relationship, no great institutions in our society and no great achievements have resulted from merely giving a fair day's work for a fair day's pay. Greatness has always been a result of employers and employees exceeding the limits of this relationship.

The performance investment, by contrast, exceeds the limits of the traditional work relationship. Teachers and principals give more than one can reasonably expect. The rewards associated with the participation investment are extrinsic in nature. Teachers, for example, are provided with such benefits as salary, retirement provisions, fair supervision, good human relationships, and security. These are the things that they can reasonably expect as the employing institution meets its basic commitments to its workers. The performance investment, by contrast, is induced by opportunities to experience deep satisfaction with one's work. This reward structure is decidedly more intrinsic.

Emphasizing Symbols and Meaning

In traditional management school administrators are encouraged to practice situational leadership, carefully calculating behaviors and strategies in a manner that reflects the characteristics of the situations they face and the psychological needs of the people with whom they need to work. There is value in situational leadership and it should be practiced, but in many schools too much attention is given to the instrumental and behavioral aspects of school leadership and life and not enough to the symbolic and cultural aspects. This attention is driven by a behavioristic view of the world. Greatness cannot be tapped, inspired, or enhanced by management practices that emerge from this tradition.

The philosopher Susanne K. Langer reminded us, "Symbols and meaning make man's world, far more than sensation."[7] The author Thomas Carlyle noted, "It is in and through symbols that man consciously or unconsciously, lives, works and has meaning." By its very nature the human species engages in and thrives on the construction of meaning. Indeed life's quest is basically the search for meaning. Leadership that counts provides symbols that count and these in turn help humankind in its quest for meaning. As James Quinn points out, "The role of the leader . . . is one of orchestrator and labeler: taking what can be gotten in the way of action and shaping it—generally after the fact—into lasting commitment to a new strategic direction. In short, he makes meanings."[8] The educational administration theorist Thomas B. Greenfield believes that "The task of leadership is to create the moral order that binds (leaders) and the people around them."[9] When leaders seek to add value to their situational leadership practice they emphasize symbols and meaning.

Emphasizing Purposing

The concept of vision gets a great deal of play in leadership literature these days. In his study of successful leaders Warren Bennis found vision to be critical. His leaders had "the capacity to create and communicate a compelling vision of a desired state of affairs, a vision that clarifies the current situation and induces commitment to the future."[10] Vision is important and valuable. Indeed leaders who are remiss in expressing and articulating a vision, in communicating values and dreams they hold dear for the school miss the very point of leadership. However, the vision of a school must reflect the hopes and dreams, the needs and interests, and the values and beliefs of teachers, parents, and students as well. In the final analysis it doesn't matter so much what the principal believes; it is what the school stands for that counts.

The key to successful schooling is building a covenant comprising purposes and beliefs that bonds people together around common themes and that provides them with a sense of what is important, a signal of what is of value. A covenant is a binding and solemn agreement by principals, teachers, parents, and students to honor certain values, goals, and beliefs; to make certain commitments to each other; and to do or keep from doing specific things. It is the compact that provides the school with a sense of direction, on the one hand, and an opportunity to find meaning in school life, on the other. Value-added leaders bring to the school a vision but focus on the building of a shared covenant. The two together comprise the leadership dimension of purposing.

Emphasizing Enabling of Teachers and the School

In July of 1986 the Education Commission of the States issued a report entitled *What Next? More Leverage for Teachers.* In that report Bernard Gifford, Dean of the School of Education at the University of California, Berkeley, stated, "If we are ever going to make a dent in the problems we face in public education, we're going to have to find ways of permitting talented teachers to play a much larger role. We need to find ways of giving talented people, first rate professionals, extra leverage."[11] This report along with others issued by the Carnegie Foundation,[12] the National Governors Association,[13] the Brackenridge Forum for the Enhancement of Teaching,[14] and dozens of other groups interested in quality schooling represents a significant turn in America's school reform policy. The key to making things better is to enable teachers—to give them the discretion, the support, the preparation, and the guidance necessary to get the job done.

Enabling teachers is an important aspect of value-added leadership; but more important than teacher empowerment, or for that matter than enabling principals or any other specific group, is enabling the school. It is principals, teachers, parents, and students together who will make the difference in the struggle for building quality schools.

Value-added leaders do not fall into the trap of equating enabling and empowerment with *laissez-faire* management. Whenever one speaks of enabling the key question that must be answered is enabled to do what? Enabling strategies make sense only when they are linked to the purposes and the requirements for teaching and learning that are implied when a shared covenant emerges in a school. The following "rule" applies: "Principals and teachers are free to do the things that make sense to them providing that the decisions they make embody the shared values and requirements for teaching and learning that comprise the school's covenant." Schools need to be linked similarly to districts, and districts to states, as part of a larger covenant that defines values that are shared by more extended communities. Enabling and empowerment have less to do with rights and more to do with responsibilities. Placing the major emphasis on the school site links rights and responsibilities together firmly.

Emphasizing Accountability

The American public cannot have it both ways. Politicians and legislators, school boards and school administrators cannot prescribe in detail what it is that teachers and principals are to do and how they are to do it on the one hand and then hold them accountable on the other. In some states, for example, well-intentioned reformers have provided the schools with regulations and requirements that are so detailed that very few decisions are made by principals and teachers about what to teach, when, and how. Arthur Wise of the RAND Corporation points out that trying to run the affairs of schools by remote control results in legislated learning, and in bureaucratic teaching and administration.[15] Academic excellence always suffers under these conditions; standardization is the great friend of mediocrity but the enemy of imagination and excellence. Furthermore, legislated learning and bureaucratic teaching make it impossible to hold individual teachers and principals and individual school communities accountable. They can only be held accountable for results when they have the responsibility for deciding the means.

Monitoring teacher performance and monitoring school performance are not substitutes for true accountability but only processes that are subsumed under accountability. Understood in this light, monitoring has value. In value-added leadership monitoring is transcended in favor of true accountability.

Emphasizing Intrinsic Motivation

Traditional management theory is based on the principle "what gets rewarded gets done." It makes sense to base motivational strategies and practices on this principle; but when this principle becomes the overriding framework for making decisions about how to lead and how to encourage and reward good performance the result is the opposite of that which is anticipated. In the long run, the job just doesn't get done. The problem with "what gets rewarded gets done" is that it results in calculated involvement of people with their work. When rewards can no longer be provided the work no longer will be done. Work performance becomes contingent upon a bartering arrangement rather than being self-sustaining because of moral principle or a deeper psychological connection. A better strategy upon which to base our efforts is "what is rewarding gets done." When something is rewarding it gets done even when "no one is looking"; it gets done even when extrinsic rewards and incentives are scarce or nonexistent; it gets done not because somebody is going to get something in return for it but because it's important. The power of intrinsic motivation is well documented in both research and practice and is a key element in value-added leadership.

Emphasizing Collegiality

Traditional management practices are based on such ideas as POSDCoRB, unity of command, "if you can't measure it you can't manage it," regulating the work flow, monitoring, and so on. These ideas are designed to provide a rational system that provides workers with directions as to what to do and controls to ensure that these directions are followed. A cousin to these traditional management ideas is the "Mary Poppins" principle. Since most people don't like to be managed in this way it becomes necessary to provide "a spoonful of sugar" to help wash this unpleasantness down. For this reason human relations management is not an alternative to traditional management but its country cousin. As enterprises are managed traditionally it is necessary to work to ensure that morale is kept up.

The emphasis on human relations management has resulted in the value of congeniality becoming very strong in the way schools are managed and led. Congeniality has to do with the climate of interpersonal relationships in an enterprise. When this climate is friendly, agreeable, and sympathetic, congeniality is high. Though congeniality is pleasant and often desirable, it is not *independently* linked to better performance and quality schooling.

For example, in the Organizational Climate Description Questionnaire studies that were popular in the sixties it was found that congeniality was high in both "open" and "closed" schools.[16] Congeniality can work positively in one school but negatively in another. It all depends on whether the foundation for friendship, agreeableness, and sympathetic understanding comprises values and beliefs that are aligned with quality schooling or values and beliefs that compete with quality schooling. For this reason value-added leaders understand that congeniality alone misses the point.[17]

Collegiality has to do with the extent to which teachers and principals share common work values, engage in specific conversation about their work, and help each other engage in the work of the school.[18] Value-added leadership views congeniality as a by-product of building strong collegiality norms in the school and not as an end in itself.

Emphasizing Leadership by Outrage

Is it important for students to come to school? Wilma Parrish, the principal of Western Middle School in Alamance County, North Carolina, thinks so. She has been known to drive to absent students' houses to find out why they missed and on occasions to drag them back to school. It should come as no surprise that attendance at Western is about 98 percent. Wilma Parrish is a remarkable principal with a nose for quality and a determination to succeed; and when things aren't right she is quick to get them fixed. Joan Lipsitz studied the Western Middle School as part of her research on successful schools. She describes Wilma Parrish as a person who is a ahead of and behind her teachers, constantly leading and prodding. She has high expectations for teachers and communicates them clearly. As Lipsitz notes, "The significantly less dedicated of her classroom teachers have come to know the results of not meeting her standards. In such cases, RIF (reduced in force) probationary teachers stay RIF, and tenured but inadequate teachers know that tenured means exactly what it is legally supposed to mean: they will be fairly evaluated and then dismissed through proper due process. In one instance, a tenured teacher resigned because the pressure from Mrs. Parrish to perform became too great, the rewards too few. In another instance, a teacher with twenty-three years' experience who had become incompetent was fired. One way or another, the message from the principal to achieve excellence in the classroom is clear."[19]

Wilma Parrish practices leadership by outrage. Despite standard prescriptions in the management literature that admonish leaders to be cool, calculated, and reserved in all that they say or do, she brings to her practice a sense of passion and risk that communicates to others that if something is worth believing in then it's worth showing passion over. In his extensive studies of successful leaders Peter Vaill found that their leadership practice was characterized by time, feeling, and focus. Leaders put in extraordinary amounts of time; had very strong feelings about the attainment of the system's purpose; and focused on key issues and variables.[20] Key in his analysis of this time-feeling-focus triad is the importance of feeling in linking together the other two. He found that successful leaders care deeply about the system, its purposes, structure, conduct, history, future security, and underlying values and commitments. They care deeply enough to show passion, and when things were not going right this passion often takes the form of outrage.

Leadership by outrage is a symbolic act that communicates importance and meaning and touches people in ways not possible when leadership is viewed entirely as something objective and calculated. For this reason its use over issues of purpose defined by the school's shared covenant adds value to leadership.

The Dimensions Together

None of the dimensions of value-added leadership, considered alone, is powerful enough to make the difference in bringing about quality education in America. Indeed a critical connectedness exists among the characteristics and dimensions, and value-added leadership is best understood as comprising interdependent parts. Practicing enabling leadership, for example, without practicing leadership that emphasizes purposing and the building of a covenant, is more likely to result in *laissez faire* management than in quality schooling. Furthermore, emphasizing management at the expense of leadership by providing controls and regulations, by emphasizing authority, by attempting to regulate the flow and work of schooling will not allow the practice of convincing and meaningful empowerment. A school that builds a covenant comprising technical statements of objectives, targets, and outcomes that fail to inspire; that are devoid of symbolic representations; and that do not allow principals, parents, teachers, and students to derive sense and meaning from their school lives will fail.

In his address "The Four Simple Truths of Management," Donald M. Kendall, CEO of Pepsico, Inc., illustrates the interdependent nature of value-added leadership dimensions.[21] The "truths" he offers are as follows: Complex organizations are best managed on a decentralized basis. However, decentralization only works when there is a central purpose to the entire organization—"a central plan against which all the separate elements can be gauged. But the development of specific objectives that support this central plan—and the development of the specific strategies, products and programs—these are the responsibility of the operating units." Kendall believes that it is important to give people "the freedom to operate within broad guidelines, not within the narrow confines of a detailed program dictated by top management. . . . The job of senior management, then, is to measure results, monitor progress and help the operating people take corrective action wherever necessary." Kendall's lynchpin for keeping everything together in a nonbureaucratic organization is top management's ability "to create a vision of the organization, a sense of purpose, everyone knows what it was that made the organization successful in the past, and what it will take to ensure the continuation of that success." This covenant needs to provide meaning to those in the organization. "All of us want meaning in our lives beyond a paycheck, beyond daily sustenance, we want the opportunity to share great values and great visions—and to have a real part of turning these values and visions into reality." Emphasizing leadership, the performance investment, symbols and meaning, the building of a shared covenant, and school site empowerment and accountability, therefore, are a package deal. When intrinsic motivation, collegiality, and leadership by outrage are added to this package we have value-added leadership in action.

Corollary 1: Building in Canvas

In describing the difference between administrative theory and administrative life the noted organizational theorist James G. March stated, "The way we talk may sometimes be less sensible than our administrative behavior—the way we act."[22] As successful leaders have come to learn, the talk of administration is the way one gets legitimacy;

and legitimacy, in turn, gives one freedom to act. The action of administration is the way one gets results. Schools and other organizations in our society operate in an open environment within which they are expected to respond to the images and expectations of sponsors. If they are successful, sponsors provide the needed support for them to function and the discretion to function freely. Schools, for example, are sponsored by powerful state bureaucracies that provide a host of expectations that they operate in bureaucratic ways. Paper must be filed, data must be accumulated, teachers must be evaluated according to rules, schedules must be followed, and so on. These bureaucratic values are sometimes reinforced by rule-happy and top-heavy local school districts' central offices. If local school leaders follow these rules to the letter, excellence remains out of reach and basic competence is endangered. If they do not follow, they find themselves in trouble at the hands of a vindictive bureaucracy.

The challenge is to reflect the images and values of bureaucratic sponsors on the one hand and to make the decisions that count for excellence in schools on the other. The answer is to build bureaucratic systems in canvas.

The latest innovation in U.S. military technology is a line of folding tanks constructed of canvas and designed to serve as decoys on the one hand, and to create an illusion of strength on the other. Building in canvas is not a bad idea when tinkering with the structure of schooling.

Schools have multiple and often conflicting purposes that make exact alignment of structure and purpose difficult, if not impossible. In the real world schools must look the way they are supposed to. To obtain legitimacy the school must be able to communicate to its sponsors a feeling of competence. In return it receives needed statements of confidence. Because of their relative remoteness, bureaucratic sponsors are attracted to the general features of school structure rather than to the details of how these features are being interpreted in day-to-day schooling. Therefore, schools have a surprising amount of freedom as they interpret policies and rules in ways that support sensible teaching and learning.

If schools master the art of building in canvas, they are able to provide the right public face thus gaining the freedom to interpret, decide, and function in ways that make sense.

Corollary 2: Emphasizing Moral Leadership

Creating illusions and building in canvas raise obvious moral questions in the minds of many. Some might argue that such ideas are deceptive and have no place in the lexicon of leadership. Moral questions, however, are not raised when school leaders are being sensitive to such human realities as loose connectedness of school parts, competing preferences and interests, the need for people to construct their own reality, and the importance of norms and values. Instead moral questions are raised when school leaders ignore these realities by continuing to push ill-fitting management theories. An immoral approach to leading is attempting to shape human nature to fit one's theory. A moral approach would be to use a theory that fits people better in the first place as the basis for school improvement.

Not only must management and leadership theory fit human nature, but it must enhance teaching and learning and other dimensions of the school's covenant as well. Bureaucratic theories of leadership are secular. They seek a response from the human mind and hand. But the unique human response is one of spirit; and our spirit responds to values, beliefs, moral dimensions, and standards. Moral leadership taps the spirit. How credible is the leader? Is the leader honest, forthright, and sincere? Does the leader model beliefs, live purposes, exemplify standards? In essence what does the leader represent, and does this representation symbolize something of value to followers? In value-added leadership authority takes on moral characteristics.

Moral questions about leadership are unavoidable. Whenever there is an unequal distribution of power between two people, the relationship becomes a moral one. Leadership involves an offer to control. The follower accepts this offer on the assumption that control will not be exploited. In this sense leadership is not a right but a responsibility. Its purpose is not to enhance the leader but the school. Leaders administer to the needs of the school by being of service and providing help. The test of moral leadership is whether the competence, well-being, and independence of the follower is enhanced as a result of accepting control and whether the enterprise of which both are a part ultimately benefits. In schools that means teaching and learning are enhanced and the developmental needs of students are honored.

Leadership combines management know-how with values and ethics. Leadership practice, as a result, is always concerned with both what is effective and what is good; what works and what makes sense; doing things right and doing right things. As school-improvement projects are considered questions of what is good, what makes sense, and what is worth doing deserve equal billing with questions of effectiveness and efficiency. When the two sides of the ledger are in conflict leaders will be known by the side they emphasize. For these reasons moral considerations are both the beginning and the end of value-added leadership.

3

The Four Stages of Leadership for School Improvement

Bartering: Leader and led strike a bargain within which leader gives to led something they want in exchange for something the leader wants.

Building: Leader provides the climate and interpersonal support that enhances leds' opportunities for fulfillment of needs for achievement, responsibility, competence, and esteem.

Bonding: Leader and led develop a set of shared values and commitments that bond them together in a common cause.

Banking: Leader "banks the fire" by institutionalizing improvement gains into the everyday life of the school.

The leadership route to school improvement is not an either (value) or (valued-added) proposition. It comprises four stages with both value and value-added leadership playing appropriate roles. Leader can begin the process at any of the stages depending upon the preceding stages that are or are not in place. Principals of "turnaround" schools, for example, typically began their quest for excellence at the first stage. By contrast, principals of schools that are functioning compentently, but not to full potential, begin the quest at stages two or three. The stages are illustrated on page 31.

In 1978, James MacGregor Burns wrote a book that has shaped the way leadership is now understood by leadership theorists.[1] His ideas, for example, are formative in such best sellers as Peters and Waterman's *In Search of Excellence*[2] and Bennis and Nanus's *Lead-*

The Four Stages of Leadership for School Improvement

Stage	Leadership by	Dimension
1. Initiation (getting started)	Bartering (push)	Value
2. Uncertainty (muddling through)	Building (support)	Value-added
3. Transformative (breakthrough)	Bonding (inspire)	Value-added
4. Routinization (remote control)	Banking (monitor)	Value-added

ers.[3] According to Burns, leadership is exercised when persons with certain motives and purposes mobilize resources so as to arouse and satisfy the motives of followers. He identified two kinds of leadership, transactional and transformative. Transactional leadership focuses on basic and largely extrinsic motives and needs and transformative on higher-order, more intrinsic motives and needs.

In transactional leadership, leaders and followers exchange needs and services in order to accomplish independent objectives. The objectives may be related but they are separate nonetheless. This exchange process can be viewed metaphorically as a form of *leadership by bartering*. The wants and needs of followers and the wants and needs of the leader are traded and a bargain is struck. Positive reinforcement is given for good work, merit pay for increased performance, promotion for increased persistence, a feeling of belonging for cooperation, and so on.

In transformative leadership, by contrast, leaders and followers are united in pursuit of higher level goals that are common to both. Both want to become the best. Both want to shape the school in a new direction. In Burns' words, "Such leadership occurs when one or more persons engage with others in such a way that leaders and followers raise one another to higher levels of motivation and morality."[4] When transformative leadership is practiced purposes which might have started out as separate, as in the case of transactional leadership, become fused. Initially transformative leadership takes the form of *leadership by building*. Here the focus is on arousing human potential, satisfying higher needs, and raising expectations of both leader and follower in a manner that motivates both to higher levels of commitment and performance.

Leadership by bartering responds to physical, security, social, and ego needs. Leadership by building responds to esteem, achievement, competence, autonomy, and self-actualization needs. The leadership concepts associated with leadership by bartering are the development of management skills, using appropriate leadership styles, and applying the principles of situational leadership theory. The principles associated with leadership by building are empowerment, symbolic leadership, and charisma.

Burns points out that ultimately transformative leadership becomes moral because it raises the level of human conduct and ethical aspiration of both leader and led thus it has a transforming effect on both. When this occurs transformative leadership takes the form of *leadership by bonding*. Here the focus is on arousing awareness and consciousness that elevate school goals and purposes to the level of a shared covenant that bonds together leader and follower in a moral commitment. Leadership by bonding responds to such intrinsic human needs as the desire for purpose, meaning, and significance in what one does. The key concepts associated with transformative leadership by bonding are cultural and moral leadership.

Leadership by bartering, building, and bonding, when viewed sequentially, comprise stages of leadership for school improvement. Bartering provides the push needed to get things started; building provides the support needed to deal with uncertainty; and bonding provides the inspiration needed for performance and commitment that is beyond expectations. A school improvement effort becomes real only when it becomes institutionalized as part of the everyday life of the school. To this effort *leadership by banking* comprises the fourth stage of school improvement. Banking seeks to routinize school improvements thus conserving human energy and effort.[5] This conservation provides the human resources necessary to initiate new school improvement efforts in other areas.

The Stages in Action

Each of the *stages* of leadership comprise one's overall school-improvement *strategy*. However, *tactically* speaking bartering, building, bonding, and banking comprise leadership *styles* that can be used simultaneously for different purposes or people within any stage. A recalcitrant teacher, for example, will likely require leadership by bartering regardless of one's overall strategy.

The four stages of leadership for school improvement are illustrated in the leadership practices of Jane Kendrick, principal of the Henry J. Eggers Middle School in Hammond, Indiana.[6] The history of Eggers parallels a Greek tragedy. Opened in 1973 as an open-space-design school it was staffed by conscripted teachers, most of whom did not identify with open-school philosophy and few of whom knew how to teach in that environment. During the first two years the school operated along departmental lines in an open-space setting. Morale was low, staff dissension was high, student discipline was a major problem, and achievement was below par. The personnel director of the Hammond School District commented as follows, "The requests for transfers out of Eggers were very high during these years. I think the percentage of requests was the highest in my tenure in personnel." In 1975 Eggers adopted the learning community concept and organized itself into interdisciplinary teams of teachers headed by a community-teacher leader. The school and its principal took a significant step toward making Eggers successful. Unfortunately this success was short-lived. In 1976 a new superintendent was appointed and the following year the district was reorganized resulting in the moving of elementary grades K–6 to the middle school and a decided deemphasis of the learning community concept.

In 1978 the principal was reassigned. When assistant principal Jane Kendrick and the new principal arrived, their major priorities were improving student behavior, teaching performance, and standards of professional conduct. At the end of the first year the suspension rate had fallen from 170 to 84 and a sense of "law and order" had been brought to the school. As one staff member commented, "There was a big difference from one year to the next. The kids shaped up and started acting better. They were more respectful in the lunch line and didn't smart off to us as much." Another commented, "My first year at Eggers I was afraid to open my classroom door. The middle school kids ran up and down the hallways and were disruptive. They didn't seem to care if you sent them to the office or not. It was different with this administration. The students did not want to be sent to the office because they knew they would be in serious trouble."

The major responsibility for teacher evaluation and the restoration of professional standards fell to Vice Principal Kendrick. At the end of the first year Kendrick, working together with the principal, had terminated the contracts of a tenured and a nontenured teacher. A clear message about quality and standards had been delivered to students and teachers.

In 1979 Kendrick became principal (the principal during the 1978–79 year resigned because of illness). While not letting up on issues of discipline, staff performance, and professional standards, Kendrick now took aim at the concept of learning communities. To her the issue was simple. "If we are going to teach through interdisciplinary teams and have students organized into learning communities, and if we are going to have team leadership then we are going to develop these ideas so they work and they work well." She was particularly concerned about the performance of the team leaders. She believed that if teachers were assigned as learning community leaders, then they would have to accept the responsibility for providing leadership on the one hand and accountability for what was going on in the learning community on the other. She noted the following problems: "Meetings were canceled regularly or meeting locations were changed at the last minute to more 'convenient' places, such as the teachers' lounge. Often, conversations would proceed while the leader attempted to begin the meeting. Sometimes team leaders came prepared with agenda but more often they did not." As one staff member commented, ". . . I would be in a meeting to discuss a student and individual team members would begin 'shooting the breeze' often about sports events. They would seem resentful if some of us attempted to get them back on task." Though one of the original purposes of team planning time was to bring together team events and activities there was no evidence that this purpose was achieved. Though constituted as interdisciplinary teams individual teachers rarely ventured outside of their own content areas. In Kendrick's words, "The problems seemed overwhelming; there was an obvious weakness in the implementation of the interdisciplinary concept; there was a lack of purpose and driving commitment to make it work. Several problems needed to be resolved."

To solve the problems Kendrick instituted regular meeting times and regular meeting places, required team leaders to develop weekly agendas, developed and provided to team leaders written guidelines for team meetings, and mandated a weekly report from team leaders to the principal. The procedures were not arrived at through consensus or agreement but were mandated by Kendrick. She monitored team meetings firsthand and examined very closely the weekly reports that team leaders submitted to ensure that meeting protocols were being followed. The functioning of team meetings improved dramatically as a result.

Through the 1980–81 school year, team leaders began to address the issue of interdisciplinary teaching. Teams worked together to establish goals and activities, but most team members continued to work independently. Kendrick continued to emphasize the need to use interdisciplinary strategies but progress was slow. The problem, as she saw it, was that team leaders still viewed their roles as being managerial—concentrating on discipline, hall behavior, rules and regulations, and similar concerns rather than on improving teaching units, the development of instructional strategies, the coordinating of teaching, and the academic progress of students. She believed that their role needed to evolve from manager to true team leader. This resulted in her emphasizing team development.

Kendrick became acquainted with the SIP (School Improvement Process) model developed by the Institute for the Development of Educational Ideas. She decided that this process was the means by which team development would be facilitated. During the 1983–84 school year Kendrick, a teacher and parent were trained in the use of the model; and in January of 1984 the project was introduced to the Eggers Middle School. Key to the SIP concept is that the building site be the basis for all school improvement and that ideas and decisions should emanate from the bottom through collaborative efforts. The SIP model begins with the school visualizing what is the "best we can imagine for our school" and then focuses on issues of ownership, governance, and program improvement. The purpose of SIP is to create a culture that views decision-making as a shared responsibility and opportunity. "Everyone affected by a decision should help make the decision."

After the three-member team was trained and the idea introduced to the faculty, an SIP planning committee was selected. This group included twelve teachers, two administrators, and five parents. As the planning process unfolded the school became committed to being "the best we can imagine." It adopted the following as its ultimate goal: "The community of Henry W. Eggers School is committed to excellence in education. Our priorities during the next five years will assure that our school is recognized as one of the best in the country." The following goals were adopted:

> One hundred percent involvement of staff, students, and parents in the educational program as evidenced by instructional practices, student achievement, conduct, and attendance.
>
> Enthusiasm and commitment to processes of instruction that will lead to attainment of mastery by all students.
>
> Consistency of behavioral and academic standards within teaching teams and among teaching teams.
>
> Commitment to the processes identified to diagnose and prescribe to various learning styles.
>
> Consistent and conscientious follow-through with academic prescriptions for various learning styles, learning strengths, and learning weaknesses.

The introduction of the SIP process to Eggers resulted in the initiation of a variety of school-improvement projects and the development of a climate of cooperation and commitment that transformed the school. In 1984 the school made a commitment to focus future improvement efforts on activities that were directly related to the needs of young adolescent learners. The school received a $20,000 grant from the Lilly Endowment Middle-Grade School Recognition Project to help in its efforts. The standardized test scores for the eighth grade that appear below provide testimony to this transformation as do the numerous awards for excellence the school has earned in recent years.

Jane Kendrick described her leadership as evolving from an emphasis on bartering to building and then to bonding. "Instead of a school culture and leadership behavior that was concerned almost

8th Grade Standardized Test Scores[7]
Comparisons at Eggers Middle School 1977–1986

	Iowa Test of Basic Skills		Stanford Achievement Test				Comprehensive Test of Basic Skills			
	1977	1978	1979	1980	1981	1982	1983	1984	1985	1986
Vocabulary	7.1	7.5	7.7	8.6	8.4	8.3	8.7	8.6	8.6	8.7
Reading Comprehension	7.2	7.5	8.1	8.0	7.9	8.4	8.6	8.6	9.0	8.9
Spelling	—	—	7.6	7.7	8.0	8.7	8.7	9.3	9.4	9.7
Math Computation	6.4	6.5	6.7	7.1	7.3	7.6	8.3	9.6	9.8	10.0
Math Concepts	6.4	6.8	7.2	7.3	7.4	7.4	7.9	—	9.5	9.5
Social Studies	—	—	—	7.3	7.7	7.6	7.8	8.9	10.0	9.6

exclusively with safety and security, I now participate in a culture that makes decisions about program based on the developmental and social, as well as academic needs of young adolescents. . . . For the most part, the transition . . . was sequential, with certain skills and actions serving as stepping stones to the next level of more complicated behavior." When Kendrick became principal in 1979 her behavior was mainly directive. "I lectured, I told people how to think, when to think, and what to think. I made up the rules, and I enforced the rules. My actions became: tell, regulate, delegate and evaluate." Later she was to emphasize coaching behaviors in an attempt to upgrade her team leaders and build each of the teams of teachers into models of effectiveness.

Adoption of the SIP and an increased emphasis on staff development in the processes necessary for implementing SIP leadership by building provided the foundation for Eggers to emphasize leadership by bonding. Her strategies during this period were to build a common purpose, create a vision, create a leadership team, provide opportunities for teachers to become leaders, and develop the value of collegiality which enabled leadership to be shared as teachers, parents, and students were recognized as partners. In 1987 Kendrick stated, "I have observed the transformation of the norms of our faculty from those which centered around safety and discipline issues to those which center around issues of moral integrity."

Kendrick believes that as Eggers moves ahead she will have to become the "keeper of the vision" motivating and encouraging faculty in their efforts to do the right things for students. She notes finally that "Several of the faculty, and particularly members of the peer leadership team, have gone far beyond what would normally be expected in their own professional development. As they have become leaders in their own right in staff development, peer coaching, and futures planning, I must realize the inevitable—that some of these individuals are going to surpass me, not only in terms of specific skill expertise, but also in terms of overall leadership ability."

The stages of leadership illustrated in the Eggers story evolved sequentially, suggesting that school improvement always begins at the bartering level. This would not be the case, however, with schools that are already functioning at a higher level. It is not likely, for example, that Kendrick will have to resort to leadership by bartering as her strategy anymore as new school improvement ventures are undertaken.

Exhibit 3–1 provides an overview of the four stages of leadership for school improvement, their links to transactional and transformative leadership, and their consequences for competence and excellence in schooling. Let's now turn our attention to the question: "Why does value-added leadership work?"

Exhibit 3–1 The Stages of Leadership and School Improvement

Leadership Type	Leadership Styles	Stages of School Improvement	Leadership Concepts	Involvement of Followers	Needs Satisfied	Effects
Value (Transactional) Leadership	Leadership as "Bartering"	*Initiation* (push) Exchanging human needs and interests which allow satisfaction of independent (leader and follower) but organizationally related objectives.	Management skills Leadership style Contingency theory Exchange theory Path-goal theory	Calculated	Physical Security Social Ego	Continual performance contingent upon parties keeping the bargain struck. "A fair day's work for a fair day's pay."
Value-added (Transformational) Leadership	Leadership as "Building"	*Uncertainty* (muddle through) Arousing human potential, satisfying higher needs, raising expectations of both leader and followers that motivates to higher levels of commitment and performance.	Empowerment Symbolic leadership "Charisma"	Intrinsic	Esteem Competence Autonomy Self actualization	Performance and commitment are sustained beyond external conditions. Both are beyond expectations in quantity and quality.

Exhibit 3–1 (continued)

Leadership Type	Leadership Styles	Stages of School Improvement	Leadership Concepts	Involvement of Followers	Needs Satisfied	Effects
	Leadership as "Bonding"	*Transformative* (breakthrough) Arousing awareness and consciousness that elevates organizational goals and purposes to the level of a shared covenant and bonds together leader and followers in a moral commitment.	Cultural leadership Moral leadership Covenant	Moral	Purpose Meaning Significance	
	Leadership as "Banking"	*Routinization* (remote control) Turning improvements into routines so that they become second-nature, thus allowing full attention to new challenges, new improvements.	Procedures Monitoring Institutional leadership	Automatic (as long as things work, people work)	All needs are supported	Performance remains sustained

Why Value-Added
Leadership Works

Value-added leadership works for four reasons:

1. *It provides the necessary latitude that enhances choices in an otherwise bureaucratic and political world of demands and constraints.*

2. *It is aligned with a realistic view of how schools and other enterprises actually work, thus its practices are practical.*

3. *It is based on a theory of human rationality that enhances both individual and organizational intelligence and performance.*

4. *It responds to higher-order psychological and spiritual needs that lead to extraordinary commitment, performance, and satisfaction.*

Reason One: Latitude

Rosemary Stewart describes managerial jobs "as consisting of an inner core of *demands*, an outer boundary of *constraints*, and an in-between area of *choices*."[1] Demands are the things that school leaders must do. If they fail to do these things, sanctions are invoked that imperil their continuing on the job. Demands are determined by school outcome specifications, legal requirements, bureaucratic rules and regulations, and the role expectations of important others such as superintendents, school board members, teachers, and parents. Constraints are the things that school leaders must not do or cannot do. They are determined by norms and values that exist in the community or school, availability of human and material resources, union contracts, school space and equipment limits, and the capability limits of teachers and others with whom school leaders must work. As with demands if school leaders ignore constraints, sanctions are invoked and their jobs are imperiled.

Though two principals may be subject to identical demands and constraints their leadership practices vary nonetheless. Within any demand-and-constraint set there are always choices—opportunities to do the same things differently and to do things one is not required to or prohibited from doing. It is in this area of choices that the opportunities for excellence are born. Whether these opportunities flourish or not depends upon the latitude that leaders are able to make for themselves.

Value-added leadership can provide the necessary latitude that enhance choices in an otherwise bureaucratic and political world of demands and constraints. Hinsdale, Illinois, school superintendent Ronald W. Simcox, for example, was faced with a school board who wanted to close a substandard, outmoded, and underutilized elementary school and with a school-community comprising subgroups uniformly unwilling to be bussed elsewhere. Conflicting demands and constraints severely limited his choices. He found the necessary latitude by setting up an open-enrollment magnet program in a neighboring school. The program was named the "Walker Model Education Center." In his words, "My vision was to establish a new visionary, growing-edge kind of program that would allow parents and students to opt for a new and different alternative program and to provide a facility. The model education center, where we could try any new exciting programs that came along would fit this bill." At the end of the first year of operation few of the parents who had enrolled children in the magnet chose to leave and over 100 students from the school that needed to be closed transferred to the magnet. This allowed the school to be closed without fuss.

Superintendent Simcox relied heavily on such value-added leadership ideas as choice, empowerment of parents, school site empowerment, and symbolism in establishing the Walker Model Education Center as an alternative. The title of the magnet school itself suggested that it was different. He marketed the school as being on the "cutting edge" and referred to it regularly as a "lighthouse." Once designated as being special the school found it easier to become special. Latitude increased as a result. Indeed the school was so successful that it provided an opportunity to springboard an open enrollment program for the entire school district.

Other value-added leadership concepts function similarly in providing the latitude that stretches one's choices while diminishing demands and constraints. The constraints found in union and association contracts, for example, can be diminished by building norms of collegiality and by constructing a shared covenant for the school that bonds together teachers and administrators in a common cause. The unprecedented cooperation between teacher organizations and administrators and school boards in Dade County, Florida; Rochester, New York; and Hammond, Indiana; for example, testify to the power of collegiality and shared purpose. Teacher commitment and performance can be enhanced by emphasizing intrinsic motivation in making curriculum decisions and in designing the work of the school. These and other value-added practices lead to extraordinary results. Once a school or district begins to achieve extraordinary results, politicians and other pressure groups have no choice but to back off, further diminishing demands and constraints.

Steve Johnson, the principal of the Mark Twain Middle School in San Antonio, found the latitude he needed to turn a problem into a solution by practicing value-added leadership. He faced the common problem of not having enough space to accommodate students at lunch within the existing schedule. His solution was to create a mentoring program for students. Every adult in Mark Twain who is willing to volunteer (and most do including the principal and custodians) has 15 students for 20 minutes each day for a mentoring session. Each mentor decides how to structure the session but the emphasis is the same—the students' problems, successes, interests, and concerns. Mentoring provides the needed latitude in an otherwise tight lunch schedule but more importantly helps students and makes an important symbolic statement about their worth.

Reason Two: Practical

Traditional management theory is based on a view of how schools operate that does not fit the real world very well. When leadership practices are based on this view they don't work the way they are supposed to. Traditional management assumes that individual schools, school districts, and state systems of schooling are "managerially tight and culturally loose." According to this theory, what counts in improving schools is management connections not people. When this is the case, the operation of schools resembles the mechanical workings of a clock comprising cogs and gears, wheels, drives, and pins, all tightly connected in an orderly and predictable manner. This is the "Clockworks I" theory of management.

Clockworks I leaders believe that the purpose of leadership is to gain control and regulate the master wheel and the master pin of their clockworks organization. This is sometimes done by introducing such ideas as a highly sequenced curriculum that is prescribed in detail, a testing program that narrows what is taught, a supervisory system for monitoring in detail what teachers do and for evaluating their teaching behaviors in a standard way, or a program that trains teachers to implement a specific teaching model thought to represent the "one best way." Such highly refined management systems are introduced to ensure that teachers will teach the way they are supposed to and students will be taught what they are supposed to learn. Unfortunately this rarely happens—at least not on a sustained and continuous basis and not without excessive monitoring and other enforcement efforts. When such a system does work, it gets people to do what they are supposed to but not more (leadership by bartering).

Here's an example of how the Clockworks I theory works in practice. In 1984 the Philadelphia school system was justifiably concerned with inequities among schools and low standards overall. To correct this program the system embarked on an ambitious and systematic effort to overhaul the city's 264 schools.[2] A standardized curriculum for all the grades was developed that outlined in minute detail the scope and sequence for instruction in each subject and provided a pacing schedule that suggested how much time teachers should spend on each topic. In addition, uniform grading and promotion standards and protocols were developed and a new set of standardized tests carefully matched to the curriculum was introduced. Each of the 12,000 teachers in the district received a detailed booklet that outlined the skills and subject matter to be taught in every subject in every grade. A system of monitoring was introduced to ensure that teachers taught what they were supposed to and when, and that they were using the grading protocols and specifications that were provided.

The Philadelphia school officials had the right goals and intentions in mind, but they did not have the right theory in mind from which to develop effective strategies for implementing these goals. A study conducted in 1987, for example, found that the standardized curriculum and the system of monitoring were not addressing the problems intended. Instead the study found that the vast majority of teachers either ignored the mandates or adapted them to their own circumstances. According to an *Education Week* article that described this study only 11 percent of the teachers were implementing all aspects of the policy; 10 percent were following the pacing scheduled; 4 percent were following the grading guidelines; and 96 percent did not think the curriculum-based test was valuable. The article quotes researcher Gail B. Raznov as stating "high school teachers reject hyperrational, authority-mandated change efforts which deny their potential and intelligence." Professor Richard A. Gibboney of the University of Pennsylvania describes the Philadelphia effort as a "non-event." "How can you get credit for something that didn't happen?" "What we have is a presumed reform that looks rigorous and lean. It's good for image-building, because the public won't learn the difference. It's the mirage of reform."[3]

In 1976 the noted social psychologist Karl Weick wrote a seminal article for the *Administrative Science Quarterly* describing educational organizations as "loosely coupled systems."[4] He borrowed the metaphor from Stanford University's James G. March, who is recognized as one of America's most eminent organizational scientists. March and a number of his colleagues have written extensively on the extent to which educational organizations resemble organized anarchies and on the link between ambiguity and leadership.[5] These are concepts similar to loose coupling. Weick pointed out that in schools each of the parts that make up the whole are only loosely connected. What happens in one place seems to have little effect on what happens elsewhere. For example, a good deal of time and effort is spent in schools on developing curriculum. The curriculum that gets taught, however, tends not to be this official curriculum but the one that is in the minds and hearts of teachers. Administrators spend a good deal of time writing memos that often are not read or that when read are often ignored. Models of teaching are adopted but don't find their way into the classroom on a sustained basis.

Weick's observations and those of March provide an image of schools that functions like a clockworks gone awry. We might refer to this image as the "Clockworks II" theory of management—a theory of cogs, gears, and pins all spinning independently of each other. Going for the main gear and pin as a management strategy just doesn't work since they are not connected to any of the other parts. Instead the leader must rely on "cultural cement" to provide the necessary connections for coordination and control. The ingredients for cultural cement are the norms, values, beliefs, and purposes of people. Weick advises school leaders to ". . . be attentive to the 'glue' that holds loosely coupled systems together because such forms are just barely systems."[6] March similarly advises. "If we want to identify one single way in which administrators can affect organizations, it is through their effect on the world views that surround organizational life; those effects are managed through attention to the ritual and symbolic characteristics of organizations and their administration. Whether we wish to sustain the system or change it, management is a way of making a symbolic statement."[7]

The Philadelphia story and the observations of Weick and March suggest that if we want to provide realistic and practical leadership, then the traditionally accepted rule for organizational functioning must be *inverted*. Schools, school districts, and state systems of education should not be viewed as managerially tight and culturally loose but managerially loose and culturally tight. What matters most is not management connections but the beliefs, values, and norms that hold people together. Failure to recognize this inverse rule leads to the development of policies and school-improvement strategies that are costly, inefficient, and ineffective. During the 1986–87 school year, for example, the state of Texas spent approximately one-quarter of a billion dollars to implement the Texas Teacher Appraisal System.[8] Expressing his high hopes for this system, the state commissioner of education, William N. Kirby, stated, "The 1986–87 school year will mark the advent of one of the most far-reaching programs of public school improvement in Texas—the Texas Teacher Appraisal System (TTAS)." Each of the teachers in the state was evaluated four times using an instrument comprising 55 teaching behaviors (*i.e.*, the teacher: interacts with students, secures student attention, maintains pace, begins with an introduction, reinforces appropriate behavior, uses correct grammar, praises, and so on). Here is how the system works. During each fifty-minute observation, the evaluator keeps track of which behaviors are and are not displayed by the teacher, awarding points for those that are. The points are then tabulated, and the teacher with the highest score is considered to be the best.

The winning teachers on the TTAS increased their eligibility for advancement on the state's merit-pay-ladder system. By and large Texas teachers willingly "showboated" the behaviors when they were being observed. However, the question for anyone concerned about wise use of the taxpayers' dollars and genuine school improvement is, what was happening when the evaluators were not there? As you can imagine, when no one is looking, teachers teach in ways that make sense to them. Unfortunately for Clockworks I thinkers, the average elementary school teacher teaches about 1600 lessons a year not four. Spending one-quarter of a billion dollars to be sure that at least four of those lessons were done a particular way just doesn't make sense.

The Florida Performance Measurement System provides another example of why practices based on Clockworks I thinking don't work. This teacher-evaluating system operates similarly to the one used in Texas. Principals and other evaluators are trained to observe teachers, coding the presence or absence of certain teaching behaviors presumed to be linked to effectiveness. The management problem associated with the FPMS is that it confuses *can do* with *will do*. Because a teacher *can* teach the official way doesn't mean that the teacher *will* teach the official way when an evaluator is not present. The taxpayers in the state of Florida are spending hundreds of millions of dollars on the wrong thing. Value-added leadership is concerned with will do. When we pay a dollar for something we should expect to get a dollar's worth. It's sustained results that count, results that don't depend on being watched. Sustained results come when people believe in and are committed to doing something.

Despite the fact that policies and management practices that are based on the Clockworks I theory are costly and ineffectual, they persist because they provide the illusion of success. Too often politicians and bureaucrats are not interested in the real thing and settle for this illusion. If teachers are being vigorously evaluated, then presumably teaching must be getting better. Rarely, for example, does one hear of a teacher getting fired as a result of being evaluated by a Clockworks I system. Bob Strode, the principal of the Finn Hill Junior High School in Kirkland, Washington, describes Clockworks I school-improvement remedies as application of the Rubber Glove Theory of Management. "If you have a leaky pen, put on a rubber glove. Your pen will still leak but your hand won't get dirty!" It is time for us to adopt management theories that actually fix our leaking pens and do not merely provide us with an illusion of success. Value-added leadership can get the job done. It has the power to influence events and people in a loosely connected world. It can provide that cultural glue that unites people where it counts—in their attitudes and beliefs. It can bring people together to work toward common goals. It can bring about extraordinary commitment and performance.

Reason Three: Rational

Webster defines *rational* as "showing reason; not foolish or silly; sensible." This is a good definition to apply to school-management and leadership policies. The key word in this definition is *showing*. A school-management and leadership policy must be judged rational or not based on demonstrated evidence. Too often, however, rationality is determined on the basis of how a policy sounds or appears and not on whether it fits the real world or works in that world.

The Clockworks I theory of management, for example, looks and sounds rational but does not fit very well the situations found in most schools; and when it is applied anyway it cannot be judged rational. This theory frames the way one thinks about planning in a single and linear direction. Without fail, ends should determine ways, and both ends and ways should determine means. First, decide on what you want to accomplish. Then figure out the best ways, the cleverest paths that will logically and effectively lead to your ends. Finally, give attention to the people who will travel the paths. Figure out how you are going to orient, direct, train, motivate, and monitor them so that they will follow the right paths. This is the right approach for situations that can be accurately characterized as managerially tight and culturally loose; but it is the wrong approach for the vast majority of situations that are culturally tight and managerially loose. Similarly this is the right approach when schools are not performing in a satisfactory way. Tightening up things in a management sense can get people to do what they're supposed to; but it is a wrong approach when the issue is striving for excellence. It is an approach that does not fit the nature of human rationality.

Theories of school management and leadership are based on different images of human rationality. When a school leader chooses a theory from which to practice, a particular image of rationality is assumed whether or not it fits the real world. A better fit between theory and practice will occur by starting the other way around. Choose the image of rationality that fits the real world first and then find a theory that fits that image of rationality.

Stanford University professor Lee Shulman provides three images of human rationality, each described briefly below. All three are true to a certain extent but some are more true than others. It makes a difference which of the three or which combination of the three provides the strategic basis for one's leadership practice.

1. Humans are rational; they think and act in a manner consistent with their goals, their self-interests and what they have been rewarded for. If you wish them to behave in a given way, make the desired behavior clear to them and make it worth their while to engage in it.

2. Humans are limited in their rationality; they can make sense of only a small piece of the world at a time and they strive to act reasonably with respect to their limited grasp of facts and alternatives. They must, therefore, construct conceptions or definitions of situations rather than passively accept what is presented to them. If you wish them to change, engage them in active problem solving and judgment, don't just tell them what to do.

3. Humans are rational only when acting together; since individual reason is so limited, men and women find opportunities to work jointly on important problems, achieving through joint ef-

fort what individual reason and capacity could never accomplish. If you want them to change, develop ways in which they can engage in the change process jointly with peers.[9]

The first image of human rationality fits traditional management theories very well. The second and third images, by contrast, are better accommodated by the Clockworks II theory of management and value-added leadership. Within the second and third images rationality is achieved by helping people to make sense of their world. As making sense builds, limits on rationality are overcome. The ability to make sense builds when people are able to construct their own definitions of situations and are involved with the leader in active problem solving. The limits, however, are too great for anyone to do it alone. Thus one key strategy for sense-building is the pooling of human resources, and the fostering of collegial values in an effort that expands individual reason and capacity to function.

When exercising leadership in accordance with the first view of rationality the leader emphasizes, in order, ends, ways, and means. First establish your objectives. Then, given your objectives, develop a plan that includes the proper management protocols for obtaining goals. These protocols should help figure out the best ways, the clearest paths that will logically and effectively lead to your ends. Next marshal your human resources. Figure out how you're going to orient, direct, train, motivate, and monitor them so that they follow the right paths. Provide the necessary expectations and the psychological support that will allow them to undertake their assigned responsibilities with ease. Ends, ways, and means assumes a certain predictability, stability, and rationality that often does not exist in the real world. It fits, for example, a world that is always managerially tight and culturally loose; but when the world is managerially loose and culturally tight ends, ways, and means does not work well. Furthermore, this view of planning places too much of the burden for school success on the principal or the designated leader. It becomes the leader's job to set the system up, to command compliance, and to provide the necessary controls to ensure compliance.

In a managerially loose and culturally tight world one needs to plan in reverse. Ends-ways-means must become means-ways-ends. Planning in reverse is consistent with the second and third images of rationality. Without losing sight of one's overall vision the leader first emphasizes means, then moves to ways, and finally to ends. Harvard

Business School professor Robert H. Hayes points out, "An organization that takes a means-ways-ends approach to strategic planning assumes everybody is responsible for its prosperity. Its success rests on its ability to exploit opportunities as they arise, on its ingenuity and on its capacity to learn, on its determination and persistence."[10] When planning in reverse the emphasis is on development of people, on building their talents and commitments, on linking them to colleagues so that together they are able to accomplish more, on encouraging their minds and hearts, and helping their hands. Once human resources are built up in both skill and heart then the school is better able to acquire and develop new and better ways to function, to create opportunities, and to exploit circumstances in a manner that results in more effective school performance. Because of the unpredictability of the world and the limits of human rationality, it makes sense to emphasize building capabilities of people and then to encourage *them* to develop the ways and means for using their capabilities, than it does to develop detailed plans first and then to seek the know-how and commitment from people to implement the plans.

Planning in reverse is consistent with value-added leadership, and value-added leadership is consistent with the second and third images of rationality. One of the reasons that the Japanese are ahead of us when it comes to commitment and performance at work is their view of human rationality. William Brown points out, for example, that in the American workplace, "Men are pegs which must be fitted into pre-existing holes. Once a man's area of responsibility has been marked out it becomes his territory. . . . The Japanese workforce, on the other hand, might be compared to a jigsaw puzzle. Compared with the polished pegs the individuals seem very irregular, 'irrational.' But the pieces themselves, through their intimate knowledge of one another's peculiar shape and coloring, fit together neatly and a clear picture emerges."[11] Value-added leadership can get the results we want in a jigsaw world.

Reason Four: Responsive

Leadership as bartering responds to physical, security, social, and ego needs of people at work. In his well-known motivation-hygiene theory the work psychologist Frederick Herzberg pointed out that these needs and the job factors that accommodated to them had less to do with commitment and performance beyond expectations than with meeting basic job requirements.[12] He pointed out that should the needs not be met, then worker performance and commitment are likely to fall below a satisfactory level; but when the needs are met all that will result is that workers meet basic job requirements. When such job factors as opportunities for achievement, challenge, responsibility, recognition for one's accomplishments, opportunities to demonstrate competence, and similar job factors were present, then such higher-order needs as esteem, competence, autonomy, and self-actualization were likely to be met. These factors and needs are related to leadership by building. They are the bridge that leader and followers must cross together as they move from ordinary performance to performance that is beyond expectations.

Sustained excellence, however, requires a still further journey. As James MacGregor Burns pointed out, ultimately this kind of leadership becomes *moral* in that it raises the level of human conduct and ethical aspirations of both leader and led and thus it has a transforming effect on both.[13] When this occurs transformative leadership takes the form of leadership by bonding. Here the focus is on arousing awareness and consciousness that elevates school goals and purposes to the level of a shared covenant that bonds together leader and led in a moral commitment. Leadership by bonding responds to such higher needs as the desire for purpose, meaning, and significance in what one does.

How do people at work respond to building and bonding leadership? In his exhaustive tests of Burns's leadership theory, Bernard Bass identified five leadership factors and assessed their effects on worker performance and commitment.[14] The factors were charismatic leadership, consideration, intellectual stimulation, contingent reward, and management by exception. Charismatic leadership was concerned with the faith and respect followers had in the leader and the inspiration and encouragement derived from their association with the leader. Consideration comprised items themed to the concern, attention, encouragement, and support the leader provided. Intellectual stimulation referred to the leader's ability to force followers to rethink ideas and to look at problems in new ways. The items comprising contingent reward were similar to the concept of leadership by bartering. Management by exception was concerned with providing leadership only when problems arose and practicing *laissez faire* leadership otherwise.

Bass found that charismatic leadership was most strongly associated with increased commitment and with performance beyond expectations. This variable was measured by such items as "makes me do more than I expected I could do; motivates me to do more than I originally expected I would do; heightens my motivation to succeed; is an inspiration to us; inspires loyalty to him or her; and inspires loyalty to the organization." Charismatic and intellectual stimulation had the strongest combined effects on motivating followers to extra effort. Charismatic leadership was the factor more strongly associated with inspiration; and charismatic leadership, individualized consideration, and intellectual stimulation were more strongly associated with loyalty to the organization than were the other factors.

The work of James MacGregor Burns and Bernard Bass are part of a growing consensus among leadership theorists in both corporate America and American education that if we aspire to excellence then value-added leadership ideas need to provide the basis for our management strategies and leadership practices. Value-added leadership works not only because it can move the hand but because it is responsive to the mind and heart. In the next few chapters we move to the question of how value-added leadership is practiced in schools.

5

Purposing: The Building of a Covenant

Harvard Business School professor Abraham Zaleznik believes that "The failure of American management is the substitution of process for substance."[1] His view applies as well to schools. Both our corporate and school leaders rate A's on such administrative processes as time management, budgeting technology, systems analysis, tactical planning, auditing and alignment strategies, and appraisal systems. They are also skilled at the matching of leadership styles to situations and the application of other human engineering techniques. The value of these management processes to school effectiveness should not be underestimated, but such processes are not substitutes for substance. It is important, for example, to know how to get from A to B, and sound management can help. However, the substance of administrative leadership is concerned with whether B is better than A and why. Furthermore, having determined the direction, substance is the means by which one brings together divergent human resources, inspires commitment, and achieves extraordinary performance. Management processes alone turn workers into subordinates. Substance, by contrast, builds followership. Subordinates comply with management processes and the leader's directives. The job gets done. Followers respond to ideas, ideals, values, and purposes; and, as a result, the job gets done well.

Chester Barnard stated in his 1938 classic book *The Functions of the Executive:* "The inculcation of belief in the real existence of a common purpose is an essential executive function."[2] This is the function that must be recaptured for American education. The inculcation of belief comes from the embodiment of purpose as leaders act and behave or from "purposing" in the words of Peter Vaill. He defines *purposing* as "that continuous stream of actions by an organization's formal leadership which has the effect of inducing clarity, consensus and commitment regarding the organization's basic purposes."[3]

Vaill conducted extensive studies of high-performing systems (HPS) (organizations that, given their resources and previous history, are performing well beyond expectations) from a broad spectrum of American society. He examined the characteristics held in common by these systems and the kind of leadership found within them. Vaill found that key to success was the presence of purposing. "HPS's are clear on their broad purposes and on near-term objectives for fulfilling these purposes. They know why they exist and what they are trying to do. Members have pictures in their heads which are strikingly congruent." He continues, "Commitment to these purposes is never perfunctory, although it is often expressed laconically. Motivation as usually conceived is always high."[4]

When purposing is present in schools the expectations of those who are responsible for the system are clearly communicated; a policy framework exists to guide strategic decision making; a value framework exists which enables daily routine activities to take on special meaning and significance; norms are established that suggest what to do and what not to do; an identity for the school emerges to help differentiate it from other schools; and as a result, the school is transformed from a secular workplace to a sacred enterprise. In describing schools recognized as excellent by the Department of Education during his administration as Secretary of Education, William J. Bennett stated "these schools make clear that there is nothing mysterious about their shared ethos of achievement. . . . These are good schools, solid places conveying sound, straightforward messages about hard work and citizenship." Though purposing is strong in these schools, Bennett believes that they are the exception rather than the norm, "Too many American schools are merely plodding ahead without clear purpose or firm grasp of the broader values and principles central to real achievement."[5]

Purposing is a key characteristic in the findings of others who have studied successful schools. This research establishes the importance of shared goals and expectations and approved modes of behavior that comprise a strong school culture. Important to this culture are the norms and values that provide a cohesion and identity and that create a unifying moral order from which teachers and students derive direction, meaning, and significance. One example is Joan Lipsitz's study of four successful middle schools: The Noe School in Louisville; the Western School in Alamance County, North Carolina; the Dorothy L. Fisher Magnet School in Detroit; and the Shoreham-Wading River School in Shoreham, New York. She found that:

> The four schools achieved unusual clarity about the purposes of intermediate schooling and the students they teach.
>
> The schools made powerful statements, both in word and practice, about their purposes. There is little disagreement within them and little discrepancy between what they say they are doing and what they are actually doing. As a result everyone can articulate what the school stands for.
>
> These are confident schools. Each one stands for something special, whether it is being the best in the county, desegregation, diversity, or the arts. Each has a mission and knows what it is and in each case it is both academic and social.
>
> In every case, a principal . . . took hold of the possible for definition and proclaimed it within the school and throughout the community. Each school became special.
>
> Made to feel like chosen people, staff and students have banded together in their specialness and achieved accordingly. The sense of definition that comes from the exclusivity felt by each school is important in keeping staff morale high and retaining parent support. More important, though, is the sense of purpose it gives the young adolescents. It helps bind them to the school.
>
> Each of the four schools has or has had a principal with a driving vision who imbues decisions and practices with meaning, placing powerful emphasis on why things are done as well as how. Decisions are not made just because they are practical but for reasons of principle.[6]

Purposing involves both the vision of the leader and the covenant that the group shares. The notion of leader vision is widely accepted but the effect of purposing on school excellence falls short if this is where it ends. Covenants provide the value-added dimension needed for extraordinary performance.

Vision gets the most attention in the leadership literature. Leaders, according to the noted leadership theorist Warren Bennis, need to have "the capacity to create and communicate a compelling vision of a desired state of affairs, a vision . . . that clarifies the current situation and induces commitment to the future."[7] Vision is an important dimension of leadership and without it the very point of leadership can be missed. However, the vision of the school must also reflect the hopes and dreams, the needs and interests, the values and beliefs of everyone that has a stake in the school. Ultimately it is what the school stands for that counts.

In their book *Passion for Excellence* Tom Peters and Nancy Austin point out that vision should start with a single person and suggest that one should be wary of "committee visions."[8] This is good advice. Principals and superintendents have a responsibility, even obligation, to talk openly and frequently about their beliefs and commitments, their hopes and dreams, their values and ideals. They are the ones who are responsible for starting the dialogue about what the school stands for, believes in, and about where the school or district should be headed.

The development of a vision, however, should not be construed as a strategic plan that functions as a "road map" charting the turns needed to reach a specific reality that the leader has in mind. It should instead, as Diamond Shamrock CEO William Bricker points out, be viewed more as a compass that points the direction to be taken, that inspires enthusiasm and that allows people to buy into and take part in the shaping of the way that will constitute the school's mission.[9] The fleshing out of this vision requires the building of a shared consensus. The building of a consensus about purposes and beliefs creates a powerful force that bonds people together around common themes, on the one hand, and that provides them with a sense of what is important and some signal of what is of value, on the other.

In successful schools consensus runs deep. It is not enough, for example, to have worked out what people stand for and what is to be accomplished. A binding and solemn agreement needs to emerge that represents a value system for living together and that provides the basis for decisions and actions. This binding and solemn agreement represents the school's covenant. When both the value of vision and the value-added dimension of covenant are present teachers and students respond with increased motivation and commitment and their performance is well beyond the ordinary.

As the school covenant is built the leader's behavioral style becomes less important than what the leader stands for and communicates to others. It is important for school leaders to do something. It
is also important to be someone—to have ideas, values, and beliefs
about what is right and good and what is worth accomplishing. The
realm of purposing, vision, and covenants is that of the high ground
that inspires and provides moral leadership. This realm should not be
confused with the stating of technical objectives and the development
of tactical plans for their implementation. The "technical" and "high
ground" mix in purposing and planning are illustrated below:

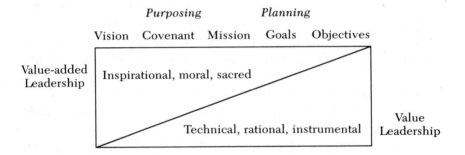

Purposing is concerned with vision (leader's hopes and dreams),
school covenant (shared values and expectations), and the *development* of the school's mission (shared purpose). By contrast, planning
is concerned with *defining* the mission and developing goals (strategy)
and objectives (tactics). Purposing is an expression of leadership and
planning a management function.

Leadership, according to General Motors training manager Ralph
Frederick, "creates vision and energy"; while management directs
resources and channels energy created by leadership.[10] In this light,
plans are important for they help guide the day-to-day activities of the
school. Raising test scores in reading on the Iowa Test of Basic Skills,
for example, is an important outcome of schooling but it hardly speaks
to school purposes. Purposes are much more inspiring, urgent, and
sacred. Planning represents the rungs on the ladder that must be
climbed, but purposes speak to where the ladder leads to.

Michigan State University professor Jay Featherstone made the
point recently that if we want to highlight the importance of schooling
it might be a good idea to mention to students and their parents, "Look,

we are taking all this trouble with you (students) because you are going to run the country someday."[11] If the school's mission was indeed to get kids ready to run the country someday, then it would need to get them ready to:

> Take charge of our cultural heritage and cherished ideas as embodied in the academic knowledge that comprises our history, literature, mathematics, the arts, and other disciplines.
>
> Provide the capital needed to support our health, commerce, educational, cultural, military, and other critical institutions; thus ensuring that we will live with safety, in dignity, and with grace.
>
> Break new frontiers in the sciences and the arts that will result in newer and better ways for us to live together and work together.
>
> Make wise decisions as wards and stewards of our democratic society.
>
> Find dignity, meaning, and happiness in their lives as they assume adult roles of parent, spouse, child, and friend.
>
> And finally, to take responsibility for their own personal health and for the health of others.

In a sense these purposes of schooling comprise a litany of sacred responsibilities that students must be prepared to undertake *and* a set of sacred responsibilities for those in the schools who have to get them ready.

Marva Collins, the founder of Chicago's West Side Prep, had a vision that revolutionized the lives of her students. Her school was founded in a basement with a handful of disadvantaged children as students. A recent U.S. Department of Education publication spoke of Collins's vision as follows: "Her vision of what they could become transformed socially maladjusted children who could not read or write into winners of statewide educational awards, into 'citizens of the world,' who saw education as their way out of poverty. The 'school creed' that she wrote embodies the vision that made West Side Prep a success: 'My success and . . . education can be companions that no misfortune can depress, no crime can destroy, and no enemy can alienate. Without education, (one) is a slave. . . . Time and chance come to us all. I can be either hesitant or courageous. I can . . . stand up and shout: "This is my time and my place. I will accept the challenge." ' "[12]

Not only should statements of school purpose sound good, they should influence the direction that the school takes and the decisions that parents, teachers, students, and administrators make as they travel in the appropriate direction. Purposes with the following characteristics are most likely to have the greatest influence:

1. They are clear enough so that you know you are achieving them.

2. They are accessible enough so that they can be achieved with existing resources.

3. They are important enough to reflect the core values and beliefs that are shared by those with a stake in the school.

4. They are powerful enough that they can inspire and touch people in a world that is managerially loose and culturally tight.

5. They are focused enough and few in number so that it is clear as to what is important and what isn't.

6. They are characterized by consonance. Most of the purposes hang together as a group. Contradictory purposes can be managed.

7. They encourage cooperation within the school and not competition. Cooperative purposes encourage people to work together by allowing each member to share in what the group achieves or attains. Everyone benefits when anyone is successful. Competitive purposes, by contrast, pit one person against another. Each member receives rewards independent of the success of the group and contingent only upon his or her own performance regardless of how well the group does.

8. They are difficult enough to evoke challenge and cause people to "gambare," to persist.

9. They are resilient enough to stand the test of time and thus are not easily changed.

Some school covenants include an operational platform that provides the rules and standards for living and working together. This is the approach being considered by the Alliance for Better Schools. The Alliance is comprised of the Hawthorne Elementary School and the

Mark Twain Middle School in the San Antonio Independent School District; the Jackson-Keller Elementary School and Lee High School from the North East Independent School District; Trinity University and the Psychological Corporation. The Alliance schools are committed to guaranteeing academic excellence for all students and are trying to identify the conditions needed for excellence. They want their platform to serve as a basis for evaluating decisions that teachers, principals, and others make. Decisions would be okay providing that they are consistent with the conditions for excellence. No decision would be allowed that was not consistent with the conditions for excellence. The Alliance schools have the following platform under consideration:

The Alliance for Better Schools is committed to the principle that academic excellence applies to all students and everyone can achieve excellence if conditions are right. Conditions for excellence:

1. *Form follows function.*
   Schools exist to promote and provide for teaching and learning. Thus decisions about organizing for schooling, scheduling, faculty assignments, curriculum, and teaching should reflect and facilitate this purpose. By contrast, decisions based on political expediency, bureaucratic convenience, or predetermined conceptions of management practice result in function following form and should be avoided.

2. *Innovation and risk taking are encouraged and rewarded.*
   Academic excellence involves inventing new solutions to old problems, viewing old problems in different ways, and confronting new problems swiftly and effectively. It is better to try and fail than not to try at all. Mistakes are okay providing that we learn from them.

3. *Reflective teaching is encouraged and nurtured.*
   Academic excellence requires that teachers develop teaching strategies and change teaching strategies in response to situations they face. Different students, different goals and objectives, different subject matter content, and different teaching contexts all require different strategies. Teaching is situationally specific. Excellence does not come in a can. No seven steps to heaven exist. No list of generic teaching behaviors can provide the magic answer. Instead teaching strategies are cre-

ated in use as teachers teach and reflect and teach again. Models of teaching do not prescribe but help inform reflective teaching.

4. *Teachers and administrators are motivated and committed.*
Academic excellence requires that teachers and administrators work hard and give a good deal of themselves to teaching and learning. They regularly exceed giving "a fair day's work for a fair day's pay." Motivation and commitment are enhanced when professionals are in charge of their practice, have ownership in school affairs, and find teaching and schooling to be rewarding.

5. *Collegiality is encouraged and enhanced.*
Academic excellence requires that teachers together and teachers and administrators work as colleagues. Colleagues are familiar with each other's work, talk clinically about teaching practice, share ideas, and help each other.

6. *Rewards are shared.*
Academic excellence requires that rewards for teachers be distributed cooperatively rather than individually. Reward systems need to bring professionals together not divide them; encourage them to share ideas, help and support each other not to compete with each other. Intercompetition for teachers (school to school) is okay but not intracompetition (teacher to teacher within the same school). "The success of one is the success of all and the failure of one is the failure of all," is our motto.

7. *Accountability is genuine.*
Academic excellence requires schools to be accountable. When teachers teach, students should be expected to learn. But accountability cannot be genuine unless it is accompanied by responsibility. Teachers and administrators, schools and school communities cannot be held accountable unless they are given the responsibility for making decisions about teaching and learning in the school.

8. *Standards are high.*
Academic excellence requires more than competence. Schools should be run in a competent manner. Teachers should teach

competently and students should achieve a level of acceptable competence in learning. But excellence requires that schools make a commitment beyond competence.. Good is not good enough: If we are to give more, we must expect more. If we expect more, students will achieve more.

9. *Developmental needs of students are connected to academic achievement.*
   Academic excellence requires that we give attention to the heart and soul as well as the mind. When the three are brought together, each benefits. When it comes to learning we cannot choose between what is good for a student academically and what is good developmentally.

10. *Open-mindedness and inquiry are encouraged.*
   Academic excellence requires that we be open to new ideas and search for new and better ways. Any idea should be considered if it can help us to teach better and students to learn better.

The operational platform of the Edmonton Public Schools in Alberta includes a number of "Principles of Organization" designed to communicate desired ideas and ideals about organizing and to provide a basis for evaluating decisions:

A. There are multiple criteria which may be in conflict that are considered when making and carrying out decisions.
   The Management Purposes should always be considered as major criteria when making decisions.

B. All individuals know the results for which they are responsible and how the attainment of the results contributes to the achievement of the purposes of the district.
   Performance evaluation shall be based on these results.

C. All individuals in the organization have only one supervisor.
   The supervisor:
   Sets Objectives
   Allocates Resources
   Directs Actions
   Evaluates Performance

Individuals may have a different supervisor at different times, or for different results.

All individuals shall be aware of the procedures for appealing decisions of their supervisors.

D. Channels of communication be kept as free and open as possible.

Individuals may go directly to any person in the organization for information, assistance or service necessary to achieve their results.

E. Authority for decisions be delegated as close as possible to the individuals affected by the decision.

The delegation of authority does not diminish in any way, the accountability of the supervisor.

Individuals with similar degrees of responsibility need not have similar degrees of authority. Delegation of authority can be individualized to match differing abilities to handle authority.

F. Only those individuals accountable for the results direct or reverse a decision associated with the achievement of those results.

Those individuals who are in a line relationship to other staff members are the only people who can overrule decisions of those staff members.

G. The creation of practices, rules and regulations designed to protect others from making mistakes is avoided.

Such measures tend to be designed with the least effective individuals in mind and their uniform application will tend to force all individuals to perform uniformly at the lowest common level of effectiveness.

H. All individuals in the district behave with absolute integrity in their relationship with colleagues, student and parents and when representing the district.

Individuals must not knowingly or carelessly, by omission or commission, misinform, mislead or withhold information which should be disclosed or do anything else to cast doubts upon the honesty, integrity or motives of others.

I. Each member of the leadership team actively promotes and maintains a relationship of mutual trust, confidence and respect among all district staff.

Each member of the leadership team has an obligation to actively pursue the foregoing with respect to all staff under that person's supervision.

The principles complement the district's Educational Philosophy, Management Purposes and other "operational platform" dimensions.

Sometimes the heart and soul of a school's covenant comprises a commitment to a set of ideas and beliefs or "theory" about the nature of schooling. This is the case in the Key School in the Indianapolis, Indiana, School District.[13] This school is the first in the nation organized around Harvard University psychologist Howard Gardner's theory of "multiple intelligences." Gardner proposes that humans are possessed by seven relatively autonomous intellectual competencies: linguistic and mathematical (the two now emphasized almost exclusively in schools), musical, spatial, bodily-kinesthetic, and two personal intelligences (one focusing on self-understanding and the other on the understanding of others). The Key School is designed to give all seven of these intelligences equal emphasis through the use of an interdisciplinary curriculum. Thus the curriculum provides a generous dose of instruction in reading, mathematics, science, and social studies. But in addition, according to Key School principal Patricia J. Bolanos, "Children should have an opportunity at least part of the day to do things they really flourish in." Thus opportunities are provided for students to "play the violin, speak Spanish, move their bodies to music, enter data into a computer, and solve board games that emphasize spatial skills."[14] Belief in a common approach to teaching and a common conception of human potential is the key element that bonds together the Key School faculty into a common cause.

The Primrose Elementary School in Somers, New York, is committed to the concept of building an intentionally inviting school—an idea advanced by William Purkey, the cofounder of the Alliance for Invitational Education. An intentionally inviting school is one within which educators consciously shape their behaviors and the environment of the school to invite students' success. A broad-based commitment to this idea within the school has implications for almost everything that goes on. Teachers, for example, need to be sure that the lessons they prepare and provide to students are interesting and challenging and invite them to learn. The school environment needs to extend to students an invitation to learn.

Jim Beaty, the principal of the Primrose school, believes that he can contribute to this ideal through his leadership and management practices.[15] He focuses on inviting the community, inviting students, and providing an inviting building. Here are some of the programs the Primrose School has developed in its effort to extend this broad invitation to succeed.

In an effort to invite the community: an open house is scheduled during American Education Week and parents are invited to visit the school, tour the building, and see classrooms in action. Community volunteers are solicited to work in the library, the school store, and to participate in class trips. Parents are invited to come to the school to share their skills and talents with students on Friday mornings in what is called the *sharing corner*. A realty day is scheduled to keep local real estate agents abreast of what's going on in the school and packets of information are provided to house-hunting families. Parental communication is enhanced through a newsletter, a parent handbook, meet-the-teacher night, regularly scheduled parents' conferences, news releases, a student newspaper, and a monthly edition of the school district newspaper. Cookouts are scheduled, with teachers and administrators helping with the cooking and entertainment. Family nights are provided whereby students, families, and other community members are invited to observe demonstrations in gymnastics, view the computer lab, visit the art rooms, and view exhibits. Adults in the community are surveyed for talents and invited to come to the school to share their talents and resources. The school chorus performs at local shopping centers and nursing homes at special times of the year. Parents are given a report card which enables them to evaluate, comment on, and provide constructive criticism of the school.

In an effort to invite students' success, there is a welcome party for new students and parents held during school hours. On the first day of school, children are met at the door of the school and escorted to their classrooms. Volunteer mothers ride the buses during the first three days of schools to ensure that new kindergarteners get off the bus at correct bus stops. If no parents are there to receive the child, he or she is brought back to school. No child is returned to an empty home. Parents are encouraged to help celebrate children's birthdays with cupcakes and other refreshments. Each month student birthdays are announced on the PA system and a record of "Happy Birthday" is played. Summer birthdays are announced in June. An after-school enrichment program is provided that includes ballet classes, Dad's Club football, baseball, and soccer. Art from a different class is featured each week in the principal's office. The principal also visits classes regularly to read to students. Stickers are placed on the work displayed in the hallways to improve the self-image of children.

In an effort to provide an inviting building, the school cafeteria has been changed to a luncheon theatre in order to provide a more inviting place to eat. Plants enhance the principal's office, the school office, and the main lobby. Classrooms are painted in soft pastel colors. The media center opens up into the hallway and has attractive displays of children's work that are changed periodically. Coffee is provided in the morning for all the staff. There is a student-sized bulletin board hung at eye level for notices and displays. Custodians are required to have people skills as well as custodial skills. The PTA provided funds for landscaping thus enhancing the beauty of the school.

Each one of these programs and practices taken alone seems small; but when brought together they communicate a special message that invites students, parents, and teachers to participate in extraordinary ways. However, one has to have a compelling message to communicate in the first place and that message comes from a shared covenant that bonds people together.

In *The Empowered Manager,* one of the most important books on leadership to appear in recent years, Peter Block provides some helpful tips on how to begin to tackle the job of creating a "vision."[16] He uses the term vision *broadly* as I do *covenant* to communicate not only the leader's vision but the amalgamation of visions that exist among members throughout the organization and that bonds them together in a common cause. Here are Block's tips:[17]

"Tip No. 1: Forget About Being No. 1."
Block believes that a vision statement should express "the contribution we want to make to the organization, not what the external world is going to bestow upon us." He believes that a vision of greatness needs to comprise a statement of what the organization intends to offer to the clients or customers it serves and to the people who work in the organization. For example, when the Psychological Corporation

launched two new companies, Learning and Teaching and HBJ Leadership, it did so with the intent that the two would become the best of their kind. But in describing his vision for the companies the president Tom Williamson didn't say "it is our goal to be number one in the field, to make more money than anyone else, to dominate the market" and so on. Instead his vision was "to increase the number of competent people in the United States by 10 percent." He wasn't concerned about recognition for the companies but about their contribution to society. Williamson agrees with Block's statement "If we get rewarded for making the vision happen, we will accept the recognition gracefully—but this is not why we pursue it."

"Tip No. 2: Don't Be Practical."
Block points out that in our pragmatic culture we are apt to think about vision in terms of the setting of specific and measurable objectives. It has already been noted that purposing is a concept different from planning. One's vision statement is not a road map but a compass. In Block's words, "A vision of greatness expresses the spiritual and idealistic side of our nature. It is a preferred future that comes from the heart, not from the head." He believes that a practical statement acts as a restraint when the idea is to make a statement about what we want to create or become.

"Tip No. 3: Begin With Your Customers."
Our customers in schools are the students and parents we seek to serve and ultimately our society. Staying in touch with the customer was one of the most important lessons taught by the Thomas J. Peters and Robert H. Waterman's best seller *In Search of Excellence* and it has become one of the fundamental principles of management among successful corporations and businesses.[18] We should expect nothing less from schools. Block makes the point that it is equally important to give attention to "internal customers": the teachers, custodians, cooks, bus drivers, and others who do the work of the school. It is fair to say that students are not likely to be treated any better than are teachers and others.

Here are some examples of vision statements from Block's book that give us some idea as to what greatness looks like when an enterprise is dealing effectively with its customers.[19] They are readily transferable to the school.

We act as partners with our customers (parents and teachers).

We are committed to our customers' success and we encourage them to teach us how to do business with them.

Our customers leave us feeling understood.

The purpose of a sales call (student conference, parent-teacher conference) is to help the customer make a good decision.

We fulfill every promise, meet every requirement.

We have the courage to say no.

We choose quality over speed.

We don't cover up bad news.

We want everyone involved to express real feelings and stay engaged.

We want to understand the impact of our actions on our customers.

We offer forgiveness to and expect forgiveness from our customers.

Our customers are as important as our shareholders (school board). We exceed their expectations.

We don't force solutions on our customers.

Our dissatisfied customers teach us how to sell to (work with) those who currently do not use our service or product.

"Tip No. 4: You Can't Treat Your Customers any Better than You Treat Each Other."

A covenant should not only communicate what is important and provide a sense of direction, but it should also indicate how people are to work together and treat each other within the school. There are many reasons for this with the most important being that students are not likely to be treated any better than are teachers. As Block points out, "If we, as customers, are being ignored, they as employees are probably being ignored. If they are cold, indifferent, and unresponsive, we have some very good clues as to the management style of their supervisors."[20] The point is that teachers and other school employees need to be treated in the very same way that we want our students and parents to be treated.

"Tip No. 5: If Your Vision Statement Sounds Like Motherhood and Apple Pie and is Somewhat Embarrassing, You Are on the Right Track."

Block believes that a great vision is characterized by three qualities: It comes from the heart; the enterprise alone can make the statement and it is personal enough to be recognizably part of that enterprise; and it is dramatic and compelling. Visions are statements of hope and idealism. They are simple, moral in quality, and compelling.

The degree of loftiness of a school vision needs to reflect where the school is on the road to excellence. For example, if the issue is achieving basic competence then an appropriate vision statement would be one that spells out more specifically the details to be accomplished. Johnson City, New York, provides an example. According to an *Educational Leadership* article written by Tom Rusk Vickery, Johnson City had to overcome a "norm of underachievement." He writes, "Johnson City bears the imprint of George F. Johnson, once head of the Endicott-Johnson Shoe Company, whose family name graces the town, the school district, and three of the four schools. Until his factory closed in 1960, George Johnson used to come to the high school to dissuade students from any aspirations for college; if his shoe factories were good enough for their parents, he told them, they were good enough for them."[21]

This legacy has been overcome and Johnson City students now post test scores that are well above the national average. Eighth graders, for example, score at the eleventh-grade level in both reading and mathematics. Johnson City committed itself not only to success in the basics but to the ideas that students should have high self-esteem as both learners and persons; should be able to function at high cognitive levels and not just on standardized tests; should be good problems solvers, communicators, and decision makers; should be competent in group processes and accountable for their own behavior; should be self-directed learners; and should have a concern for others.

To achieve these goals Johnson City adopted a number of operating principles that provided the basis for making decisions about all aspects of school life. Instructional leadership, for example, was to become the first and foremost responsibility of everyone. "Every aspect of school life is subject to change *if* that change increases the probability of achieving the district's desired outcomes." The district became obsessed with aligning everything that it did with these simple aspirations. A good attendance policy, for example, was one that supported the instructional program. School board policies were evaluated to be sure that they were consistent with the school's vision. In a sense anything goes providing it fits what it is that the school is about. As Vickery points out, "Someone—a teacher or an administrator—will identify an instructional practice that promises to solve an existing problem or to improve achievement in some way. If it is consistent with the beliefs and practices of the district then several people will learn all they can about it, usually by going to a training program at district expense. Then, with better knowledge of the practice, district staff will evaluate it in terms of its appropriateness for the district."

A great deal can be learned about how to move from vision to covenant by examining two of the best kept secrets of leadership: the benefits of seeking the competitive advantage and of adopting a marketing orientation—the topics of the next chapter.

6

Seeking the Competitive Advantage

The benefits of seeking the competitive advantage and of adopting a marketing orientation are well known in the private sector but not appreciated much in education. Competitive advantage, according to Harvard Business School professor Michael E. Porter, "grows fundamentally out of the value a firm is able to create for its buyers." In business, value may take the form of prices for equal benefits that are lower than those of a competitor or "the provision of unique benefits that more than offset a premium price."[1] Enterprises that are stuck in the middle and offer neither a price advantage nor unique value manage only because their survival is guaranteed and rarely function in extraordinary ways. In achieving the value of unique benefits, an enterprise must convince its relevant buyers, audiences, or clients that what is offered is special in type and quality. This need to manage the perceptions of the value it offers leads the enterprise to adopt a marketing orientation.

The competitive advantage and the development of a marketing orientation to achieve it have obvious implications for building and maintaining support for the enterprise's product or service. Less understood, however, is how the two help an enterprise come to grips with what it believes and what it seeks to accomplish—its purposes and covenant. As purposing becomes the basis for marketing strategy, the enterprise and its employees experience a sense of pride and an enhanced feeling of self-esteem that results in increased commitment and more extraordinary performance. Seeking the competitive advantage and adopting a marketing orientation, in other words, can also help a school move from vision to covenant and to achieve extraordinary results.

Private schools are more adept at seeking the competitive advantage. Typically they take a more entrepreneurial stance. By contrast public schools are largely "domesticated" organizations with survival guaranteed (as long as the supply of students lives in the attendance area) regardless of the type and quality of service they provide. The typical private school has to provide a service that someone will "buy" if it wants to survive. This forces private schools to give more attention to such questions as, "What are we about, how are we unique, what do we believe in, what are we trying to accomplish, and are we responding to client needs?" They have to seek the *competitive advantage* in order to be successful. Within the business world one principle of marketing is that uniqueness is valued and that people are willing to pay a higher price for a unique service or unique product. Similarly, private schools try to be unique. Such concepts as vision and covenant are ways in which they work out their uniqueness on the one hand and communicate this uniqueness to potential clients on the other.

John Sommerville, the principal of Glendowie College (a public high school in Auckland, New Zealand) has learned the value of achieving the competitive advantage for his school. In New Zealand parents are free to send their children to any publicly funded school. Most opt to send their children to the neighborhood school, but many do not. Thus public schools have to be concerned about attractiveness and service to clients if they want to maintain and increase enrollment. High schools in New Zealand are allowed to set and charge nominal enrollment fees independent of government funding if they wish. Such fees provide the school with discretionary funds for various purposes. Glendowie College advertises itself as having the "Highest fees of any state school in Auckland. We have to make certain that parents get value for money." Glendowie charges parents about $65 per student a year in such fees—a modest amount by most standards, but substantial enough for the school to be concerned about giving parents and students their money's worth. In addition to this *guarantee*, Glendowie views itself as a unique school in the Auckland urban area for a variety of reasons, and strives to provide a diversified curriculum accompanied by a commitment to parent involvement and a family atmosphere. It sees itself as "a family, country school atmosphere in an urban setting."

The metaphor of writing a brochure is a good one for schools that want to adopt a "competitive advantage" as a means to tackle the task of building a covenant. If your livelihood and that of others in the school were dependent upon providing a unique and valued service to clients, and if parents could send their children to any school that they wished, what would you say to them in a brochure that would convince them that your school is the place to be? What do you believe in? What are you about? What are you trying to accomplish? Why are these values unique and important? What can parents and students expect if they opt to attend your school? This is the kind of challenge that many private schools must rise to every day. The Daybridge Learning Center, a successful national chain of daycare centers operated by ARA Services Company, has risen to the challenge. The text of its brochure appears below.[2]

Discover Daybridge

Striving for Excellence.

"Our goal is to be the most highly regarded child care and early education provider in the United States."

> Lewis Shapiro,
> President

The commitment at Daybridge is unique. Professional goals overshadow business goals. Success is defined in terms of excellence instead of dollars. From bright-eyed toddlers reaching out to touch a friendly new face to eleven year old boys and girls taking pride in assumed responsibility—these moments and years of discovery are the focus of Daybridge Learning Center.[SM] Each child has his or her own set of possibilities. We help those possibilities unfold. Our simple commitment is: Doing what's right for children.

Learning vs. Teaching.

"In early years, the learning process is much more important than the content being taught."

> Kay Albrecht, Ph.D.,
> Director of Education

Because Daybridge programs are designed to maximize individual development, our activities focus on the *process* of learning. So the emphasis is on the experiences children are having rather than what results from the activities. In other words, painting is more important than what is painted: building with blocks is more important than what is built. In very small groups, we can guide their learning as we adjust our curriculum to each child's interest and skill level.

Parents are Partners.

"Parents are the most important adults in their children's lives. Working closely with them is a tremendous help in guiding the development of their child."

Kathy South,
Center Director

Daybridge directors and teachers value their relationships with parents and demonstrate that with regular parent-teacher conferences designed to highlight each child's development. Parents are always encouraged to observe programs in action as often as their busy schedules permit. Together, teachers and parents can do what's right for their children.

The Miracle Unfolds.

"To me, the most exciting period in early development is the first 36 months. I can't imagine anything more rewarding than giving love and attention to these special young people."

Dorothy Watkins,
Infant/Toddler Teacher

Infants* and toddlers are a special delight at Daybridge. With a great deal of individual care and attention, we let their world unfold comfortably as they stretch their minds and bodies to take it all in. We stimulate without pushing. We reward with love. We insure that no child ever, ever feels alone.

*Infant care is available at selected centers

Bright Beginnings.ˢᴹ

"Preparing a child for formal education is an exceptional challenge.

When I feel confident I've taught them how to learn. I know they'll do well as they enter their school."

Jane Betty,
Kindergarten Teacher

Preschool programs at Daybridge bring the joy and excitement of learning to each child. Divided by age groups, the classrooms are designed to accommodate intimate "learning centers" where groups of three to five children pursue their interests and hone their skills. This unusual degree of personal attention allows the Daybridge preschool teacher to adjust the type of activity and pace of learning to every child. And each Daybridge child can experience success every day.

"Big Kids" Love it.

"Our before-and-after school programs provide more than fun, games, and transportation. These children are still discovering, and loving every minute of it."

Julia Cassard,
Assistant Director

Children who spend before-and-after school hours at Daybridge receive personal guidance in their continuing development. Their growing independence is understood and nurtured as they learn to accept responsibility in their maturing role. And, they have fun, to be sure. Hobbies, art and science projects and recreational activities keep them busy, active and interested.

Discover for Yourself.

"My talks with new parents always reveal a sense of relief. They saw that

*all good child care centers offered the
same services, and even talked alike! A
visit to Daybridge showed them that
there really is a difference.''*

*Bettye Ann Grice,
Educational Supervisor*

Good child care centers do offer
similar services. Safety and security,
transportation, hot meals and nutritious
snacks, appropriate teacher/child ratios,
clean and modern facilities and state
licensing. The difference is one of
attitude. And the only way to
experience an attitude is with a
personal visit.

Call now to arrange a visit to
Daybridge Learning Center. Bring your
child. We'll let you observe our
programs in action, instead of just
giving you a tour. Then, compare our
unique learning environment with
others. We're sure you'll find an
attitude that can only be expressed as
"doing what's right for children."

The Saanich School District in British Columbia discovered the bonus of the competitive advantage—a renewed sense of pride in the schools among teachers and administrators and the coming together of commitment to a common purpose after it initiated a marketing program. In 1984 Saanich found itself at a low ebb. The provincial government was making serious budget cuts in education and there was heightened criticism of schools, teachers, and student performance. Saanich school superintendent Janet Mort observed that "Our teacher morale was low because of the low public opinion of education and the lack of response by the school district and the Saanich community."

The Saanich leadership decided that rebuilding teacher morale would require a reawakening of interest in, support for, and commitment to the school by the local community. This led to the development and launching of "Project Pulse" (Public Understanding of Learning and School Education), a public-awareness campaign based on sound marketing principles. The district decided to define *public* broadly and to target the extended community as well as the school community recognizing that only 21 percent of the adults were parents of children. The nonparent majority comprised businesspersons, senior citizens, and other groups who had less interest in and knowledge about the schools. Key would be the idea that education serves society not just parents, thus all elements of the community need to view themselves as stakeholders and beneficiaries. Four-person teams comprising a parent, a teacher, a nonteaching employee, and the principal from each of the district's 20 schools attended a series of seminars on the theory and practice of marketing. The teams were responsible for spearheading the marketing efforts that would be developed in the schools.

The central office provided overall support for individual school-marketing efforts by purchasing newspaper ads that touted school successes. According to Superintendent Mort, "Although private schools have been quite freely advertising in newspapers, the public system had always felt that this would not be acceptable to the public. We decided to test this theory by putting ads in the paper with photos of outstanding students outlining their biographies and their successes in our system. These ads were very popular with the public and we actually had letters of congratulations from members of the public who did not have children in the school system saying it's about time we heard about successes of the public school system." The newspaper ads were supplemented by one-minute radio spots that focused on special programs in the district. "The radio station even developed a musical logo for us. These ads have been very popular and very powerful and play up to 10 to 15 times a day. They are less like ads and more like proud announcements." A second radio station agreed to participate in a Student-of-the-Day Award. Each school would send in nominations and the radio station would announce the daily winner. Winners received prizes from local businesses ranging from modest T-shirts and records to bicycles.

To Superintendent Mort the most significant activities occurred at the school level. "We told our schools they didn't have to do additional things to market. They simply had to ask themselves the final question in their planning for everyday activities: 'Now that we're doing this, be it a Christmas concert, an industrial arts display, or a writing fair, how will I ensure that the public beyond my parental community comes to know about it?' " Here are some of the examples of what the schools "marketed":

In the past, the Saanichton School had an annual writing fair. In marketing this program, parents took students out into the community with buckets of daffodils. Students handed out the daffodils in downtown streets along with special invitations to people they met to come to their writing fair. Several hundred additional people attended the fair that year.

The Brentwood School had an annual Heritage Day to study the history of the community. In marketing this program students took invitations to senior citizens homes and apartment buildings in the neighborhood area resulting in 800 adult visitors to the school on Heritage Day—many of them senior citizens.

At the Greenglade School, students decided to launch a campaign on buckling up seat belts in cars as part of their safety education lessons. They put up a sign on a highway overpass near the school "Greenglade students care—Honk if you are buckled up." Hundreds of people driving by honked their horns knowing that there was a school nearby with children not only learning but caring.

The dining room at Stelly's Secondary School was a teaching kitchen for vocational students. The school sponsored a special lunch for senior citizens only. "The sight of the seniors in the dining room with their bonnets on enjoying a very cheap meal cooked in a gourmet style with student waiters, hosts and hostesses touched many and impressed all." A similar story could be told about the marketing efforts of each of the other schools in the Saanich District. It represented a total commitment to touch the extended community in a highly significant way. Project Pulse was a success. Not only did the community learn more about the schools but they cared more as well, reversing a serious negative trend and building widespread support for the schools. The bonus, however, were the effects on the morale of the teaching staff and other school employees.

During the initial phases of the project many of the teachers were opposed to the notion of marketing, feeling that it was unprofessional or degrading in some way. However, as community praise and support began to mount, the schools were encouraged to be even more creative in their marketing approaches. According to Superintendent Mort, "Soon staff rooms were abuzz with the latest reactions from the senior citizens home, letters from businesses in the community thanking the teachers and students for displays and visits, and many compliments. As other teachers in the schools observed this, they too wanted to participate and soon in each school, the web grew larger and larger with people who were finding it exciting, stimulating, and rewarding. These people began to say to themselves, 'The public does care, we are doing a good job, positive things are happening, I am proud of what I'm doing, my students are successful, the community does care.'" She notes further, "We saw the change in people, as they began to believe in themselves again."

Though increases of public support were welcome results of the marketing effort, the building of self-confidence and pride in the school among staff became the key benefit. In Janet Mort's words, "Self-confidence builds, sense of pride builds. As sense of pride and self-confidence builds, willingness to take risks builds. . . . We found ourselves, after two to three years of systematic and steady marketing of our schools, as well as emphasizing the pride and successes of our system, in an environment of people who are excited, proud and open to new ideas."

Mort and her colleagues at Saanich did not limit their marketing efforts to addressing the community at large but concentrated their efforts on one particularly key element of the community—local businesses. They launched an aggressive campaign aimed at creating mutually beneficial school-business partnerships. She notes, "We went to them and said, 'We have skill and talent in our district and you have a product. We can take your product, we can use it, we can advise you on it, we can advise you on how to improve your product so it's more marketable in the education field, let's make a deal.'" Here are some of the results:

AT&T Canada provided three fully equipped technology labs, outfitted with the most advanced computers, laser disc players, video systems, and other integrated technologies for the price of two.

The Thompson newspaper chain provided the district with access to Infoglob, a newspaper data base, in six of the schools; and in return the district designed a pamphlet and brochure for them which they could use to market Infoglob to schools.

The Sony Corporation made six portapac video cameras available to the school district; and in return the district provided them with an analysis on the use of portapac for elementary students.

As a result of these ventures over $1.3 million worth of services and products were brought into the school district within a single year. Since they were not gifts but were products and services offered in exchange for something of value that the district could offer to the various businesses, a new level of respectful partnership was attained.

Superintendent Janet Mort is convinced that adopting a marketing orientation is a key link in a chain of events that leads to a greater sense of purpose, heightened commitment, and extraordinary school performance. She states, "I credit the climate in this district as well as its energy and pride to the link I found between marketing and morale, morale and positive environment, positive environment and risk free environment, risk free environment and innovation, innovation and creative ways to deal with one's problems. This cycle then repeats itself. As people become more excited and more eager the marketing begins to happen spontaneously." Key to this chain of events is the enhancement of purposes, the building of pride, and the pulling together of school and community in a common cause.

Marketing also has a stretching quality that resembles the effects of the self-fulfilling prophecy. For example, when Selden S. Edwards became headmaster of the Crane School in Santa Barbara, California, ten years ago, he found a school with low enrollment whose survival was threatened. In talking with parents of prospective students he described the school not as it was but as it could be. "About 75 percent of what I said was already in fact happening. The other 25 percent was what I hoped the school would become. I spoke about a school in which children worked hard, loved learning, and were kind to one another. Over time, the Crane school came closer and closer to this reality. Teachers picked up this theme and added conceptions not yet in place that represented their vision for the school. Emphasizing stretching not only provided a compelling portrait to parents that resulted in increased enrollment but became real allowing us to stretch again."

Many readers will justly feel uncomfortable with the advocacy of such ideas as competitive advantage and marketing orientation for public schools. Competition can be divisive and aggressive if misunderstood or misapplied. Some people, for example, advocate strategies that make teaching more competitive by providing to schools differential reward structures linked to *individual* performance. The result is intragroup competition as individuals who are supposed to be on the same team compete with each other—a misuse of the virtue of competition. Imagine a team of engineers who together are designing a new spaceship, automobile, ballistic missile, or bridge and are forced into competition with each other. They will be less likely to help each other, to share ideas, to provide support, or to pool information under these circumstances. Intragroup competition is discouraged in corporate America and should be discouraged in schooling America as well. Intergroup competition, however, when not conceived as a game of win-lose hardball, is not only fun, stimulating, and motivating but has the ability to pull people together and to enhance teamwork. These are important ingredients in any formula that seeks to build commitment and encourage extraordinary performance.

The competitive advantage and adopting a marketing orientation can help build purposing in the school. The primary reason for purposing is to enhance the sense and meaning that teachers, students, and parents experience. In the next chapter we examine the link between value-added dimensions of purpose and enhancing meaning, and show how the role of symbolic leadership helps bring the two together.

7

Symbolic Leadership: Enhancing Meaning

"All of us hunger for that which is sacred."

Sam Bellows

If purposing is to have value, it must be lived in the everyday interactions and actions of everyone in the school. The challenge of leadership is to translate values and ideas into actions and programs.
Symbolic leadership can provide the bridge between ideas developed
and ideas in use, stated values and values embodied in school practice.
John Meyer knows how to practice symbolic leadership.

In 1973 John Meyer became principal of the Garvin School in the
Garrett School District near St. Louis, Missouri.[1] Garvin, built in 1950,
had fallen on hard times. It had become known as a "combat zone,"
"the armpit of the district," and as the "dumping ground for teachers"
not succeeding elsewhere. Teachers described teaching at Garvin as
rough and a newly arrived sixth-grade teacher, assigned to replace
another who was leaving because of a nervous breakdown, was greeted
by students with "GO HOME" signs hung from his classroom windows. By 1984 the school had earned a reputation as one that not only
worked but one that worked well. The 1983 achievement test scores
at Garvin, for example, were received with disbelief by some central
office administrators. One commented that "Something must be wrong
with the tests if Garvin did that well."

Deciding that tackling all the problems at Garvin at the same time would be counterproductive, Meyer began on the road to school improvement by concentrating first on bringing about a level of competence in the areas of discipline, student achievement, and teacher performance. The result was a consistently applied discipline plan that, while demanding, had clear moral overtones. The plan was based on such basic principles as caring, praise, love, and concern coupled with high expectations and clearly defined personal accountability for one's behavior. An instructional management system was developed which involved close monitoring and coaching of teachers and teaching by Meyer. Comfortable with his knowledge of curriculum and teaching, Meyer did not hesitate to let teachers know when performance was not up to standard. He was quick to provide individual help when needed and emphasized teaching-oriented staff development programs for everyone. He refused to accept excuses from teachers when students were not learning. He helped one teacher who was having difficulty develop a plan for improvement and followed persistently to see that it was carried out, offering help as needed.

Though progress was slow and efforts time-consuming for Meyer, his pushing and persistence paid off. As one central office person put it, "John Meyer is stubborn: He will work with the teacher who has potential and won't give up. He has straightened out more staff and made good professional teachers of them. Some are on his staff now." Less promising teachers were let go or were encouraged to take early retirement.

Meyer was a superb manager with highly refined situational leadership skills. He developed, for example, a file folder system with folders numbered consecutively one to thirty-one for each day of the month. As issues, demands and other requirements crossed his desk he would decide whether to take immediate action or to mark "the item with ff23 indicating into which folder his secretary would place the task. Items are placed according to the time needed for completion." Each morning Meyer's secretary placed the day's file folder on his desk for his perusal. The contents then became the day's scheduled tasks.

Other situational leadership skills he practiced were "calculated neglect" and the use of nonverbal communications. In his words he was good at putting "things on hold, to wait and see later, to get more information. It may be defined by others as not doing the job, but eventually I get around to doing what's best. .... Calculated neglect leaves it on your mind so you can think it through." He was skilled at the subtle use of body language. When people visited the office he always gave enough time to thoroughly deal with the issues and concerns at hand but rarely gave any more. As researchers Stanfield and Walter report, "Meyer is able to get up from his chair, walk someone to the door, and end the conversation before the person realizes that the conversation is over."

Though initially many teachers were uncomfortable with Meyer's approach to leadership and the demands he was to make, the majority of staff came to respect and admire him. As time went on he delegated more of the burden of schooling to them and built a climate of caring and collegiality. Solid management and good interpersonal relationships—the raw materials of situational leadership—combined with an emphasis on coaching of teachers were the conditions that helped Meyer to secure a level of competence that would make Garvin work. He knew how to practice leadership by bartering and building.

Researchers Stanfield and Waller point out, however, that "It is obvious in this study of John Meyer and Garvin School that it required more than these (situational leadership, management and human relations) skills to cause Garvin School to be identified as a 'turnaround school' brought from the 'armpit of the district' to a school recognized for its exemplary programs and achievements." The *key* ingredient these researchers found was Meyer's ability to convincingly play the role of *principal teacher* on the one hand and to *bond* staff, students, and parents together around a common set of values and ideals on the other. This bonding would help them derive sense and meaning from their school lives and to make a commitment to excellence. Meyer was also a master at symbolic and cultural leadership, the value-added dimensions that can lead to extraordinary performance. Stanfield and Waller describe Meyer in action as follows:

> Meyer visits the classrooms, the cafeteria, the playground, and the teachers' lounge. He supports the building of traditions at Garvin and takes an active role in developing rituals that are performed daily, monthly, and yearly. He begins each day with announcements and the Pledge of Allegiance. .... He involves the families in the enterprise of schooling when he calls the parents at home or at work to inform them

that their child was the "good news" student that day. He supports the staff at Garvin with his Friday classroom visits to award pencils to the students who have completed all their work for the week. He is actively involved in the yearly reading program and involves parents in the program by requiring a signed contract agreeing that a special time will be set aside daily for reading. The annual visits of the headless horseman is another Garvin school tradition that is important to staff, students and community.

The horseman tradition was played out each year at Halloween when the headless horseman would ride across the schoolyard to the squeals and laughter of delighted children. As he galloped high on his black horse head in hand he would lift his cape to reveal his identity to everyone's delight but to no one's surprise. On one occasion Meyer, wearing a "Miss Piggy" costume complete with wig, dress, and beads, rode into each classroom of the building on a motorcycle. The purpose was to motivate students to participate in the winter home reading program. (Miss Piggy was just one of a series of characters who have been employed through the years to kick off the annual program.) Stanfield and Waller note further:

> Meyer also carefully works to construct the reality that he sees as vital for the students at Garvin to succeed. He stresses to the students the importance of using their abilities, of doing their best in all endeavors, and in realizing that one person can make a difference in their lives. They are told that they also have a responsibility to make a difference in someone's else life. He models his positive regard for the children when he stops in the hallway to hear a child's tale of weekend baseball accomplishments. He states his beliefs and models daily that the children at Garvin can learn and succeed. He is consistent in his expression of beliefs that the school can make a difference in the lives of children, and that what is best for the children should guide decision making.

Symbolic and cultural leadership can help communicate messages to parents, students, and staff that highlight the values, principles, and directions that are considered important to the leader and the school. When Bob Macklin, the principal of the Fox Lane High School in

Bedford, New York, moved his office from an interior location in the building to one that opened on a main thoroughfare of the school, he was extending an invitation to the students that his door was open.[2]

Steve Johnson, the principal of Mark Twain Middle School in San Antonio, frequently phones students who don't show up for his daily scheduled mentor group session. He phones in the evening, especially asking to talk to the missing student, not the parents. His message? "I was worried about you today—are you coming tomorrow?" Armonk, New York, Byram Hills High School principal Joseph Dipalermo tries to stand at the main entrance of the school each day to greet students and to say goodbye to them.[3] This is his way of taking to heart William Purkey's advice "Show me your greetings and show me your leave takings and I will know your relationship." The relationship Dipalermo wants for all the students at Byram Hills is communicated loudly and clearly.

Pope Crook, the principal of Castle Hills Elementary School in San Antonio, gives coupons to students that they may then exchange for hugs from staff. The "good for one free hug" coupons communicate to students that the school cares about them and help them to feel good about themselves. The coupons also communicate to staff and parents the importance of building self-esteem in students. These principals are practicing symbolic leadership. Symbolic leadership provides an important link between the school's covenant and the meaning and significance that students and teachers enjoy as part of their daily school lives.

The Forces of Leadership

Successful leadership requires that one know how to make the right choices—choices that maintain a delicate balance among competing requirements. Think of leadership, for example, as a set of forces available to principals and other school leaders as they work in the school. Five forces comprise this set: technical, human, educational, symbolic, and cultural. All of the forces are important but they play different roles in achieving extraordinary performance.

Sound management techniques comprise the power of the technical force. Proper management is a basic requirement of all organizations if they expect to function properly day by day and to maintain support from external constituents. Furthermore, poorly managed enterprises can have negative effects on workers. The noted motivation psychologist Ray C. Hackman, for example, found that "poor organization of work" resulted in such negative feelings among workers as frustration and aggression, anxiety, personal inadequacy, and even social rejection.[4] Management provides the order and reliability that makes the workplace secure and that frees people to focus wholeheartedly on major purposes and central work activities.

The human force of leadership derives its power from harnassing the school's social and interpersonal potential, its human resources. Schools are human-intensive and the interpersonal needs of students and teachers are of sufficient importance that should they be neglected school problems are likely to follow.

Expert knowledge about matters of education and schooling is the power of the educational force. This force is concerned with the educational aspects of leadership. When principals rely on the educational force they assume the role of principal teacher.

The technical, human, and educational forces of leadership provide that critical mass needed for basic school competence. A shortage in any of the three forces upsets this critical mass and less effective schooling is likely to occur. In this sense they provide value; but the presence of the three forces does not guarantee excellence.

Symbolic leadership comprises the fourth force. When expressing this force, school leaders assume the role of "chief" emphasizing selective attention to or modeling of important goals and behaviors, and signaling to others what is important and valuable in the school. Touring the school; visiting classrooms; seeking out and visibly spending time with students; downplaying management concerns in favor of educational; presiding over ceremonies, rituals, and other important occasions; and providing a unified vision of the school through proper use of words and actions are examples of leadership behaviors associated with this force.

The power of the fifth force, cultural leadership, comes from defining, strengthening, and articulating enduring values, beliefs, and cultural strands that give the school its identity over time. This is the "high priest" function of being a leader. The behaviors associated with cultural leadership include articulating school purposes and mission; socializing new members to the school; telling stories and maintaining or reinforcing myths, traditions, and beliefs; explaining "the way things operate around here"; developing and displaying a system of symbols over time; and rewarding those who reflect the culture. The net effect of the cultural force of leadership is to bond together students, teachers, and others to the work of the school in a common cause.

Building a Culture of Excellence

One of the leading experts on the topic of school culture, Vanderbilt University professor Terrence E. Deal, believes that symbolic leadership is key to achieving extraordinary commitment and performance. His book *Corporate Cultures*, co-authored with McKinsey consultant Allan A. Kennedy, provides a template for understanding the culture of an enterprise and the leadership dimensions that help strengthen this culture.[5] Deal maintains that "the pathway" to educational excellence is inside each school. It exists in the traditions and symbols that make a school special to students, teachers, administrators, parents and the community.

Deal believes that a school's culture can be strengthened by first beginning to explore and document its history. Each school has its own story of origin, of the key people that were involved, and of the circumstances that launched it. "Throughout a school's history, a parade of students, teachers, principals, and parents cast sustaining memories. Great accomplishments meld with dramatic failures to form a potentially cherishable lore. This legacy needs to be codified and passed on."[6] Deal acknowledges the importance of developing a set of core values that comprise the shared covenant for students, teachers, administrators, parents, and others. He points out, however, that this set of shared values does not appear mystically but rather evolves from the school's experience and has historical analogues. He maintains that values detached from the school's history rarely have the kind of meaning that counts.

A second step on the road to strengthening the school's culture is to "anoint and celebrate heroes and heroines." These are the figures that Deal maintains provides tangible examples of shared values and provide necessary role models for others to emulate. These people should be identified and celebrated as heroes and heroines. Examples he provides are "a teacher who turned down a corporate offer to stay in the classroom close to students; a student who learned to read despite major learning handicaps; a custodian who knows each student by name; a principal who successfully fought the district superintendent and initiated a new program for parents; or a former student who once struggled with math and caused trouble and now is a well-recognized physicist."[7]

Strong cultures, Deal points out, build traditions and celebrate rituals that testify to the importance and significance of shared values. In good schools, for example, teaching is considered to be a sacred ritual. Principals go into classes not to monitor teachers or to check up on students but to celebrate the sacred ritual of teaching, thus enhancing the meaning and significance of teaching and learning in the minds and hearts of teachers and students. Deal believes that the use of ceremonies and dramatic events are important strategies for building a school culture. Pep rallies, assemblies, and graduation ceremonies are examples that quickly come to mind. Too often these standard ceremonies become routinized and their value is then diminished. The secret is to make the ceremony as sacred as possible. Sometimes new ceremonies have to be inaugurated and old ones revamped. Very few elementary, middle, or high schools, for example, have a matriculation ceremony. This is an ancient rite designed to enroll a person as a member of a body or enterprise. Its origins are in ancient colleges and universities but the idea is readily adaptable to the modern school.

Here's how such a ceremony might work in a high school or a junior high school. The ceremony would be held in the evening so that parents could come and witness the enrollment of their children as members of the unique student body that comprises the Evergreen School. They would, of course, be dressed in their best clothes. The new students, properly attired, would then be marched into the auditorium or gymnasium taking seats up front. The stage would be filled with flower arrangements and a candelabra or two burning brightly.

At the signal, "Pomp and Circumstance" rings out over the loudspeakers and the faculty marches down the center aisle wearing their academic robes. They take positions on the stage facing the students. There would be a parade of short speeches by representatives of the local school board, the principal or principals of the sending schools, the principal of Evergreen, the president of Evergreen's PTA and so on. The superintendent in academic robes and other local dignitaries, formally attired, would be introduced and duly recongized. The students would then rise and take a matriculation oath promising to study hard and do their best to uphold the values and traditions of the school, promising not to let down their parents, promising to prepare to take their positions as those who will run the country someday. At the conclusion of the matriculation oath a well-rehearsed chorus would sing the first stanza of the Evergreen school song. The newly matriculated students would join them for the second stanza. Everyone present would sing the third stanza. Closing remarks would be made. A suitable exit song would be played as the faculty marches out, followed by the dignitaries, and then by the students. A reception would follow. The event would be covered fully by the media.

To some, a matriculation ceremony and similar events might be considered as clever tricks designed to deceive people. The noted organizational theorist James G. March would respond to such criticism as follows: "The stories, myths and rituals of management are not merely ways some people fool other people or a waste of time. They are fundamental to our lives. We embrace the mythologies and symbols of life and could not otherwise easily endure."[8] Deal believes that it is important for teachers and administrators who want to revitalize a school culture to tell good stories—vivid stories of memorable events and important accomplishments that embody the values of the school. Finally, Deal recommends that the cultural network of the school be strengthened and officially rewarded. He states, "People often wonder why the school secretary, custodian, or elderly teacher seem to have so much power. Their power usually derives from their unofficial role as priest, gossip, or storyteller. Schools need to identify these people, to integrate them into the mainstream of activity, and to reward them for the important positive contributions they make. A principal who fights the informal network usually loses; one who works with the cultural cast of characters can have a powerful effect on a school."[9]

The Semantics of Leadership

To fully understand and practice symbolic and cultural leadership the emphasis needs to be on the semantics of leadership, not the phonetics. What the leader does represents the phonetics. What the leader's actions and behaviors mean to others represents the semantics. Focusing on semantics helps in the understanding that very often it is the little things that count. One does not have to mount a white horse and charge forward in a grand dramatic event all of the time. Simple routines and humble initiatives properly orchestrated can communicate very important messages and high ideals. John Saphler, President of Research for Better Schools, and Carlisle, Massachusetts school superintendent, Matthew King, for example, point out that the content of symbolic and cultural leadership need not be different from that of technical, human, and educational leadership. In their words, "Cultures are built through the everyday business of school life. It is the way business is handled that both forms and reflects the culture. . . . Culture building occurs . . . through the way people use educational, human and technical skills in handling daily events or establishing regular practices."[10]

When practiced and understood as symbols daily routines can communicate important values and commitments. For example, Lucian Kii, the Principal Education Officer for secondary schools in the Solomon Islands, received a telegram from the headmaster of a residential secondary school located in an isolated area. The telegram stated that the school's electrical generator had broken down beyond repair. Without electricity in the faculty houses, school, or dormitories, the headmaster had no choice but to evacuate everyone from the site. Lii went to his superiors at the Ministry of Education to seek money for a new generator but was told that none was available for that purpose. All funds were already committed. Not wanting to let the school close down, Kii spent the next twenty-four hours trying to unfreeze committed funds. He found a $30,000 surplus in a dorm construction fund and decided to use this money. He then telephoned the local electric generator dealer and found that a new generator was available for $25,000 including handling and transporting. With the money earmarked and the generator identified he returned to the ministry to do a little arm-bending. The officials acquiesced and he sent a message by radio advising the headmaster that the generator was on its way. Two days later he received another telegram of heartfelt thanks from the headmaster. To many people, the Principal Education Officer's scouring of budgets, telephoning electric generator dealers, and twisting arms at the ministry may not seem to be very glamorous. But Kii's efforts sent an important message to both high officials in the ministry and to the headmaster of that secondary school— a message that schooling is important and that everyone in the ministry, and in the schools was there to serve that purpose. This kind of message gets heard by students, influencing their commitment and performance.

Leadership as Drama

James G. March emphasized the importance of symbolic leadership when he stated "administrators manage the way sentiments, expectations, commitments and fates of individuals concerned with the organization fit into a structure of social beliefs about organizational life. . . . If we want to identify one single way in which administrators can affect organizations it is through their effect on the world views that surround organizational life; and these effects are managed through attention to the rituals and symbolic characteristics of organizations and their administration."[11] According to Fordham University professor Robert J. Starratt, symbolic leadership emerges out of the leader's dramatic sense or dramatic consciousness. Symbolic leaders tend to experience life as something dramatic. They seem driven by a desire to capture the significance of the moment and to create a sense of excitement that results from seeing the dramatic possibilities for achieving important things. In his words: "When we go to the theater to see a dramatic production, we experience life within the context of the stage."[12] Being intense, stage life is able to transform ordinary experiences into larger, more meaningful ones. "Most of us experience our lives, as measured out in tablespoons, as stretching out over a dull canvas—with small joys and minor disappointments most of the time.

Routine dulls the edge of excitement, the bureaucratization of our work smothers the feeling of adventure, impersonality of social rituals distances the pain of others. The stage, on the other hand, shows us human life intensively lived. On the stage human actions and gestures appear to be enormously significant."[13]

University of Georgia professor Edward Pajak has successfully used the metaphor of drama to analyze the roles, social interactions, and leadership actions of school leaders. One of his studies was of "Eastview," a small urban school district in eastern Georgia with a professional staff of about 1300.[14] In 1982 the district faced a $6 million budget deficit and the superintendent's contract was not renewed. The new superintendent, a former high school principal promoted from within, proclaimed that the schools were "in a mess" and that he would need 100 percent support and help from the community, administrators, and teachers to overcome the crisis that Eastview faced. He "pleaded" with these groups for a "team approach" and for a "spirit of togetherness" for the sake of the children and the district. Pajak reports that the financial deficit was the first issue the new superintendent addressed. He asked the school board to invite experts from the chamber of commerce to audit the books, reviewing accounting and purchasing procedures and to make recommendations for improvement. He made more than 300 presentations at churches and meetings of civic and other groups during his first year and a half as superintendent. "The unchanging message was: 'We're in a mess. I can't get out of it alone. We need you folks. We've got to do it together.' " The superintendent announced that improvements in student achievement test scores along with school climate improvements and increased community participation would be the measure of district progress and that he would *resign* in three years if improvements were not made. He indicated to principals that they were expected to focus their attention on teaching and learning and that he would support them to the hilt; but if test scores and other indicators of progress did not increase at the building level they would be leaving the district along with him.

Pajak analyzed the dramatic events of Eastview using the thirty-six dramatic situations identified by Georges Polti. In his classic 1924 work Polti claimed to have identified the thirty-six archetypal dramatic situations that accounted for all of the plots in dramas up to that date.[15] Pajak noted that two distinct plots seemed to have been played out in the drama of Eastview. "The first is Polti's situation number six, the 'disaster: a great reversal of roles when a defeat is suffered or there is a natural catastrophe.' This might be taken as an apt description of the $6 million deficit and tradition of poor academic performance in Eastview."[16] In reversing this situation the superintendent offered to resign within three years if progress was not made. This dramatic event corresponds to the twentieth situation identified by Polti: "Self-sacrificing for an ideal." Polti considers this dramatic event to be among the most powerful noting that "none is nobler than this of our twentieth situation—all for an ideal: what the ideal may be, whether political or religious, whether it be called Honor or Piety, is of little importance. It exacts the sacrifice of all ties, of interests, of passion, of life itself. . . ."[17] The sacrifice of one's job for a matter of principle may well have carried the day in rallying the needed support for Eastview to move forward.

A. Paul Hare, in his book *Social Interaction as Drama*, points out that in everyday life ordinary people must modify the presentation of ideas in response to reactions of the listener whereas actors on stage typically follow a fixed script until the play is over. "In everyday life, as people react to an idea either positively, negatively or indifferently, some are moved to take roles in support of the idea, others to take roles that are critical of the idea, and some to remain neutral. If the idea that is presented is not the espouser's own, there may be someone similar to a playwright behind the scenes who created the idea. There may be someone who facilitates the presentation of the idea like a director. There is always a stage, or action area, where the activity takes place. Persons who are outside this action space form the audience. The time during which a presentation takes place is always limited. It may be only a few minutes or it may be a lifetime; an actor, however, cannot hold the stage forever."[18]

Dramatic plays are based on ideas that provide the needed focus for the social interactions that comprise the performance. Ideas become actions as one moves along a continuum of abstraction from image to theme to plot to script. These four points parallel the movement from *vision* to *covenant* to *strategy* to *tactics* as ideas become actions. Leaders play a variety of roles during this transformation. They assume the role of playwright who develops the image, theme, plot or script; of director who organizes the activities of others as the script is played, and sometimes of an actor who participates in the performance itself. The role of audience helps one to think about why the drama of leadership is played in the first place. What is to be accomplished and what kind of audience response is anticipated?

In drama, the action unfolds in caricature with time compressed and emotion assuming precedence over intellect. The audience, therefore, must pay more attention to the meaning of an activity than to the actual behaviors and events. Much like leadership, dramatic life is symbolic. One communicates with the audience in a semantic rather than a phonetic mode.

John Meyer, the principal of the Garvin School, was a skillful playwright, director, and actor; and his multiple role-playing suited both him and the situation he faced at Garvin. Jane Kendrick, the principal of the Eggers Middle School discussed in chapter 3, was also adept at assuming all three roles. As her leadership emphasis shifted from building to bonding it was necessary for others to assume the actor roles in the drama. Increasingly she moved behind the scenes as director and moved offstage as playwright supporting the performance of others.

Good directors, playwrights, and leaders are enablers who make it possible for others to succeed by providing the means and opportunities for action. Enabling, a key dimension of value-added leadership is the theme of the next chapter.

8

The Three E's: Enabling Teachers and Schools

The three *E*'s of value-added leadership are Empowerment, Enablement, and Enhancement.

- Empowerment is practiced when authority and obligation are shared in a way that authorizes and legitimizes action, thus increasing responsibility and accountability.

- Enablement is practiced when means and opportunities are provided and obstacles are removed permitting empowered persons to make things happen, to be successful. Unless enablement accompanies empowerment, empowerment becomes a burden and indicators of effectiveness become illusions.

- Enhancement leads to enhancement. Followers' roles are enhanced when empowerment and enablement are practiced and the leader's role is enhanced as a result. The leader's role is transformed from manager of workers to leader of leaders. Role enhancement for both results in increased commitment and extraordinary performance.

This is a chapter about bottom lines for America. When it comes to deciding how to run our schools the bottom line is: will the decisions we make and the policies and practices we implement enable teachers to teach better and schools to function more effectively? Will, for example, teachers and principals be able to make thoughtful decisions about school practice that will lead to better learning conditions and outcomes for students. Will parents be able to become the kind of partners in the education of their children that will provide more support for and better decisions about teaching and learning? Nothing else matters in the end.

The stakes are too high for us to continue our present bureaucratic course in managing schools simply because we've always done things a certain way. America needs a better quality school product to carry us into the next century. If this product is not forthcoming we will not be able to compete effectively with other high-tech economies. Obviously intellectual, social, and personal goals of schooling are prime and a singular emphasis on economic goals is both narrow-minded and shortsighted. However, the four purposes of schooling are interdependent. If America fails economically she will not have the opportunity or the resources to support the vital educational, health, military, cultural, civic, and recreational institutions necessary to guarantee a comfortable, humane, and secure future for our children. America must succeed, not just survive; and that reality makes the links between education, the economy, and the quality of life even more critical.

How must teaching and learning change for America to succeed? Kathleen Devaney of the Holmes Group and Michigan State University professor Gary Sykes believe that the schools must provide students with both old and new basics; building upon mastery of the fundamentals to emphasize reasoning, higher-order thinking, critical analysis, self discipline, inquiry, and problem solving. They believe that schooling must become much more intellectually rigorous than is now the case.[1] Center of Leadership and School Reform president Phillip C. Schlechty believes that the roles of students must change from mere collectors of facts and information to knowledge workers. Knowledge workers don't just collect information they must use it. Devaney and Sykes point out that, for students to function as knowledge workers, familiar patterns of teaching must be exchanged for new ones that emphasize intellectual rigor, problem solving, academic integrity, and thoughtful student performance.

This tougher, more complex, and challenging view of schooling cannot become a reality in top-heavy, command-oriented, bureaucratic schools where decisions about curriculum and teaching are made centrally, where teachers are viewed as workers to be directed and inspected, where teaching is conceived of as doing what someone else decides and doing it the same way for everyone, and where principals are relegated to being inspectors and managers who are responsible for ensuring that teachers do what they are supposed to. The kind of teaching needed in an information society is high-level work. High-level work teaching is complex and situationally specific. Decisions about what to do and how need to be made on the spot as the teacher interacts with students in context. Different intents, different students, different contexts, and different situations all require different decisions.

Syracuse University professor Gerald Grant believes that two changes are essential if we are to make the needed transition in schooling—both are intended to reestablish in the schools the intellectual and moral authority lost in recent years: Teachers and principals must be put in charge of their practice, and schools must be allowed to shape their own destiny. In his words, "Most teachers and principals in public schools do not feel that they control their fate. They have lost a sense of efficacy and . . . belive that they are on the receiving end of policies made elsewhere. Principals have become middle managers who process directives issued from a multilayered bureaucracy."[2]

To get the job done, a new partnership among parents, principals, teachers, and students must be created in each of our nation's schools— a partnership of shared cooperation and commitment to make the best possible decisions for quality schooling. The school itself, not the district or the state, is the key, and enabling leadership linked to accountability is the means to shape this partnership of excellence. This new partnership means that the roles of school superintendents, central office staffs, and state bureaucrats will have to change from deciders and doers to enablers. Principals and teachers in partnership with parents must, in turn, become the deciders and doers. Rochester, New York associate superintendent Jean Slattery puts it this way, enabling schools means "less bosses and more resources in the central office."[3]

Enabling leadership is empowerment and more. *Empowerment* means "to give official authority to those who work on site in the school." *Enablement* means "to provide principals, parents and teachers in each individual school not only with the opportunity but the means to succeed, to make things possible." To some, enabling principals, parents, teachers, and the school may seem like a radical idea but it is one of the most important lessons we can learn from the best of America's corporations.

Lessons from Business

The stifling effects of high-control, command-oriented, top-down bu-reaucratic management are well known to America's corporate leaders. Business endured for too long under a similar system with devastating results. Today devolution, decentralization, site-based management, shared decision making, self-management and other empowering and enabling strategies are widely practiced in corporate America. The Exxon Corporation began its restructuring in 1986. "Aimed at adapting the company to a new, more competitive era, the reorganization sig-nificantly reduced layers and thinned the ranks of upper management, while shifting more responsibility to middle managers. With a new emphasis on quality one of the goals was to get Exxon Chemical closer to its customers—essentially, building the business organization back from the customer rather than forward from the plant."[4]

In a recent speech advocating site-based management for schools, Richard D. Miller, the executive director of the American Association of School Administrators, pointed out that 240,000 administrators, su-pervisors, and central office support staff now run the nation's schools.[5] This is roughly one for every ten teachers. Few would dispute the importance of thoughtful and committed superintendents and prin-cipals to effective schooling; but one wonders whether the number of *other* nonteaching educational professionals isn't getting out of hand. Xerox Corporation CEO David Kearns believes that this is indeed the case and advocates the streamlining of central offices while beefing up the importance of school sites. "Make central office administration a service center. Go ahead and allocate funds, but the principal and staff will be responsible for spending them. Central administration should *sell* its service to the buildings—let teachers and principals decide (what services they want to buy). . . . That will streamline middle management . . . and it will put resources where they belong, in the school building."[6]

Many of our private schools function and function well on much leaner central offices. In a recent *New York Times* article, for example, Edward D. Fiske reported that 6,447 persons worked at the Brooklyn headquarters of the New York City Board of Education—a ratio of one for every 147 students. By comparison, the number of people working at the central office of the Roman Catholic Archdiocese of New York was 27—a ratio of one for every 4,200 students. There are only 18 professionals and 9 secretaries in the Archdiocese central office for 322 schools and 114,000 students. As Fiske points out the two districts cannot be readily compared and certainly not on a one-to-one basis; for the public schools must offer more and different programs and have different responsibilities. Still the ratio of 1-to-147 versus 1-to-4,200 tells us something about central office bureaucracy.[7]

How do the Catholic schools manage with such a lean central office staff? Archdiocese of New York school superintendent Brother James Kearny explains: "We see our job as helping the faculty of each school to do what is best for their particular students. . . . We'll explain to them what the Regents Action Plan says . . . but they have to flesh it out for their own school."[8] Recognizing fully that the mission and political context of the public schools does not allow for direct comparisons, Fiske is right nevertheless when he says that there are lessons to be learned here.

Empowering workers and adopting shared decision-making practices are now viewed as bottom-line strategies in corporate America. American Express's James Robinson III believes that the link between full employee participation in decision making and corporate success is direct. In his words: "The problem with excessive autocracy is that it breeds mediocrity down in and through the corporation. The more participatory you are, the more people have a chance to be full and aggressive team members."[9] John Akers of IBM believes that shared participation should encompass the full range of corporate concerns including shaping the vision. "The vision is certainly not the product of any one individual's mind . . . it's more the product of a collection of minds."[10] This theme is echoed by Proctor and Gamble chairman John Smale: "There is power that comes with the position, but executing that power is not a unilateral kind of thing. You manage a business together with other people."[11]

To Donald Peterson, the highly regarded CEO of Ford, participative management is key. He credits participative management with being the critical factor in the turnaround of the Ford Motor Company. He believes in pushing decision-making authority "as far down in the organization as we think we possibly can, on the very sound principle that the further down you get, the closer you're getting to where there's true knowledge about the issue."[12] Perhaps Judy Lechner Knowles, principal of the George Washington School in Philadelphia, sums up the bottom line on empowerment for both corporate and schooling: "Empower or be devoured."

Many American corporations are taking the concepts of empowerment and enabling leadership a step further by boldly experimenting with self-management. Since 1986 the Goodyear Tire and Rubber Company in Mount Pleasant, Iowa, has been run by "supervisorless teams" or "self-directed work groups" comprising about 150 employees. Accounting for this innovation plant manager Robert Becker comments: "I think what really happened was, as the education level and expectations of our employees grew, the workplace wasn't keeping up with their ability to function in that workplace."[13] Instead of having production managers and floor supervisors, each team chooses its own coordinator who acts as the liaison between the group and Becker. The responsibility of the liaison is to communicate problems, suggestions, and ideas but not to coordinate or supervise. Becker states, "We operate on the principle of trust and mutual respect. We trust that our employees will do what is expected of them, what is right, what is fair." What are the results of self-management at Goodyear? "They really have a fierce sense of ownership in this plant," Becker states.[14] The plant has experienced a 40 percent increase in production since the introduction of self-management in 1986, and significant drops in absenteeism and accidents as well. Furthermore, self-management has been introduced into several other Goodyear plants.

Management expert Thomas J. Peters believes that self-management may well be one of the great secrets in successfully motivating employees. He maintians that it is more successful in the long run than merit pay, a lesson learned by such users of self-management as Dana Corporation, NUMMI (the joint Toyota-GM venture), and Harley-Davidson. He states, "Achieving spirited self-management . . . is the objective. To get it, from a management standpoint, anything less than an abiding belief in the capability of the average worker will lead to unsatisfactory long-term results."[15]

The lessons from business are important. If empowerment and enabling leadership are good enough for Goodyear, NUMMI, Dana, Xerox, Ford, Harley-Davidson, American Express, IBM and Exxon then they are especially good for the Washington Elementary School, **King Middle School, and Losoya High School.**

School-Based Management

The solution to the problem of parents, teachers, and principals having too little control over the work of the school proposed by such diverse groups as the American Association of School Administrators, the National Education Association, the American Federation of Teachers, and the Carnegie Foundation for the Advancement of Teaching is school-based management. Many experiments in school-based management are now underway. Edmonton, Alberta; Monroe County, Florida; Rochester, New York; and Dade County, Florida; for example, have garnered headlines for their efforts in this direction. The Dade County collective bargaining agreement reached in July 1988 expanded initial experiments with school-based management to a larger number of schools. The agreement provided for involving teachers in helping other teachers improve their skills, selecting principals, determining curriculum materials, planning the design of staff development programs, and renovating schools. In praising the new contract, Dade County superintendent Joseph A. Fernandez commented that it was "part of our efforts to improve the workplace for teachers by returning a greater measure of involvement and dignity to the profession."[16] Individual schools in Dade County may apply to the district and union to become site-based managed. A memorandum jointly issued by Superintendent Fernandez and United Teachers of Dade vice president, Pat L. Tornillo, list the following among the criteria used to evelute applications: how the school will be accountable for success; will develop and implement collegial processes; will make shared decisions; will involve the community in decision making; and will improve the overall school climate. Furthermore, each school is expected to target the issues, practices, and procedures it intends "to change, modify or alter." The school indicates, as well, the "necessary waivers in existing administrative directives/regulations, present School Board policy, labor contract provisions, State Department of Education rules, and/or state law" that it believes will be required for targeted changes to be realized.[17]

School-based management is a key element in the new "shared governance" plan initiated in September 1988 in Easton, Pennsylvania. According to an *Education Week* report[18] the plan includes:

Allowing the presidents of the Easton Area Education Association and the Easton Area Principals Association to participate in meetings of the school board and of the superintendent's cabinet.

Forming school planning councils, consisting of a principal and two elected teachers to share decisions on curriculum, promotion criteria, discipline, and other policies.

Creating a "joint professional senate," with a principal and one teacher delegate from each school, to discuss districtwide concerns.

Establishing a joint personnel committee to give teachers a greater say in decisions on transfers, assignments, and teaching schedules.

The Edmonton, Alberta, public schools are pioneers in school-based management. Each of the schools is responsible for 75 percent of its budget, with block funds allocated according to an equity-weighted per-pupil formula. A formula also allocates the number of "full-time equivalent" employees for each school but schools are permitted to "trade in" teacher positions for two classroom aides. High schools are even allowed to drop athletic programs such as football if they choose to do so. In Superintendent Michael Strembitsky's words: "Until you give them a piece of the action, they're fighting you. Once you give it, it's a partnership."[19]

School-based management plans need to be carefully developed from the perspective of the three *E*'s of value-added leadership: empowerment, enablement, and enhancement. Otherwise they are likely to shift the locus of control from outside the school to the principal's office; creating, in effect, a chain of small dictatorships across the country. A development such as this would merely exchange one set of problems for another, with teachers and parents still having too little say over matters of schooling. As it stands now, according to a recent Carnegie study, though most teachers report being involved in choosing teaching materials and shaping the curriculum (79 percent and 63 percent of those responding) they are much less involved in other decisions affecting their work. More than half of the respondents reported not being very involved in setting discipline standards, assigning students, and designing in-service programs. Over two-thirds of the respondents reported not being very involved in setting promotion and retention standards and deciding school budgets. Finally, over 90 percent of the respondents reported not being very involved in the evaluation of teaching performance, selecting new teachers, and selecting principals and other administrators.[20] Can you imagine physicians, lawyers, accountants, engineers, and other professionals having so little say about similar issues in their enterprises? Something is wrong here.

Thankfully many examples exist of schools who believe enough in their teachers to empower them. This is what the Crane school in Santa Barbara, California has to say about its teachers: "Crane's faculty is the heart of the school. They are responsible for the design and content of the academic program and for creating an atmosphere conducive to the joyful pursuit of learning. All faculty members share responsibility for the coherence and integrity of the curriculum. . . . They are a positive and interested group of individuals who convey enthusiasm for their areas of study with quiet authority, academic depth, warm concern and a sense of humor." At Crane not only is teacher empowerment considered the right thing to do, it is the effective thing to do for when teachers are empowered they work harder and better, with improved student learning as the result.

Power "Over" or Power "To"?

The important question is how can the concept of school-based management be understood and implemented in a way that it does not become a power grab for parents, principal or teachers? Run-of-the-mill definitions of empowerment emphasize the giving of power to one group or another and this implies the taking away of power from some other group. However, empowerment can also be understood as the exchange of one kind of power for another—the exchange of *power over* for *power to*. Value-added leaders, for example, are less concerned with controlling what people do, when they do it, and how; and more concerned with controlling accomplishments—the likelihood that shared values will be expressed and shared goals achieved. These leaders realize that to most effectively accomplish the latter, one must give up control over the former. When school-based management is understood in this way, the triangle is exchanged for the circle; a top-down management view of schooling is exchanged for a moral community built upon shared purposes and beliefs:

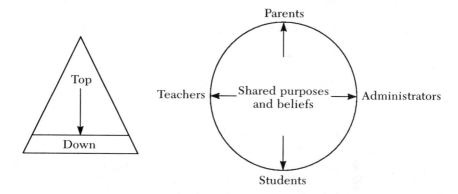

In the circle principals, parents, teachers, and students are empowered together and are enabled together to meet commitments to a set of shared purposes and values. They are driven, held together, and work together in response to a moral commitment. For this reason it is more useful to talk about empowering the school site than empowering a particular group. The idea is not so much to empower teachers, parents, or principals independently of each other but to empower the school as defined by its shared purposes and values. When this is the case, teachers and others involved are free to do what makes sense to them providing that the decisions they make embody the school's shared purposes and values—the school's covenant. When the three value-added *E*'s of empowerment, enablement, and enhancing are linked to purposing, principals, teachers, and parents respond with increased motivation and commitment as well as surprising ability.

Trading the triangle for the circle and practicing the three *E*'s changed the culture at the Montlake Elementary School in Seattle with dramatic improvements in student performance. As principal Lavaun Dennett explains:

> This new culture includes a commitment to excellence and an
> acceptance, even appreciation, of change that assures us all that this
> school will keep becoming what it needs to be. We lead one another in
> this process of becoming. Sometimes I fill that role, sometimes a
> teacher, sometimes a student, or a parent. We all have something of

importance to share. We all get an opportunity to grow and learn as well as teach and share. We continue to complete the circle only to find that there are more wonderful opportunities waiting.

The research literature on power in organizations provides strong support for directing enabling leadership to empowering the school site. The work of University of Michigan professor Arnold Tannenbaum is considered seminal. He found that leaders can actually increase control by giving up authority. Furthermore, power and influence should not be considered as zero-sum economic concepts. Sharing power means more power for everyone—power has the capacity to expand.

Tannenbaum found that the total amount of power and influence that existed in an enterprise across ranks was a better predictor of satisfaction and performance than was the relative amount of power and influence held by any one group as compared with another. His ideas apply as well to schools. Imagine, for example, two schools with influence patterns on a one-to-ten scale as follows:

School A		School B	
Parents	2	Parents	4
Teachers	3	Teachers	6
Principal	4	Principal	9
Sum	9	**Sum**	19

In School A power is fairly "equally" shared among parents, teachers and principals with a difference of one noted for teachers as compared with principals and parents as compared with teachers. In School B, the differences are three and two, thus power is distributed in a somewhat less "equal" manner. The sum of power in School A, however, is less than one-half of that for School B. Tannenbaum would predict that though the distribution within School B is less equal, B would report higher levels of satisfaction and higher levels of performance across the board. The reasoning being that school site B was more empowered than A.

How Superintendents and the Central Office Can Help

Schools are loosely connected in a managerial sense affording opportunities for daring principals to be *de facto* empowered and to practice enabling leadership even in a rigid bureaucratic system. But the full potential of enabling leadership will not be realized without active involvement and commitment from the superintendent and the school district central office.

During her years as superintendent for curriculum in South Bend, Indiana, Lynne Miller and her colleagues in the curriculum division empowered teachers and principals and practiced enabling leadership.[22] They decided, for example, that teachers should take an active role in curriculum writing, staff development, practice-oriented research and in coordinating the curriculum. They wanted to help teachers become active teacher leaders, believing that this was the way to build a professional culture with self-sustaining norms of excellence. Teachers became actively involved in producing curriculum materials and guides, working as full partners with the central office. The writing projects were ambitious and dealt with important issues that required coming to grips with purposes and values, transforming these into educational program formats, and then into practical teaching guides across a wide range of the curriculum. "It's like I'm back in graduate school, only this time the problems are real and I'm the one with the answer, not my professor," remarked one teacher who was involved in the writing projects. Another stated, "For the first time in a long time I'm using my brain. I'm debating reading topics with fellow teachers and suddenly I feel we're all very smart people." Miller notes, "By relinquishing control of the curriculum-development process, central-office administrators place themselves in a unique position to provide the opportunity for teachers to assume leadership. Once teachers 'try on' leadership, they find that it fits them like a glove. As teachers become leaders they come to . . . value themselves and they come to value each other; and in so doing they transform the professional culture in which they work."

Classroom teachers became the key designers, presenters, and evaluators of a wide range of professional development programs. Teacher-developed and -led staff development programs makes sense for a variety of reasons. First, when teachers have problems and are in need of help they turn to other teachers. Second, teachers consider ideas and insights from other teachers to be more credible than from other sources. Third, the opportunities for teacher leadership in the area of staff development enhance self-esteem, promote interaction among teachers, and provide teachers with a sense of accomplishment.

Helping teachers assume expert roles in practice-oriented research and sharing with them full responsibility for curriculum coordination registered similar results. One teacher, for example, remarked, "I knew I was a good teacher, but never knew how good I was. People listen to what I say; they ask me what to do. After you've done something for a long time you have a bag of tricks. I can open that bag and share it with other teachers. I can give help if people ask. Now, I'm an authority. This job has changed my life. It changed how I see myself and what I'm capable of doing." And another remarked, "I love having the power and authority to help improve classrooms." Helping to build teacher leadership is, for Lynne Miller, the first step toward building a professional culture of teaching.

Lynne Miller and her colleagues were successful in practicing the principle of a power investment. They distributed power among others in an effort to get more power in return. They were not so much interested in "power over" teachers and what they did but rather "power to" achieve shared goals and purposes. They understood that for this to happen teachers needed to be empowered to act—to be given the necessary responsibility that would release their potential and make their actions and decisions count. But more than just empowerment they understood the importance of practicing enabling leadership. They provided the support and the conditions that enabled teachers to be successful.

One of the most important, albeit often overlooked, players in providing the leadership needed for broad-based quality schooling is the school superintendent. Without her or his involvement and commitment bright spots will exist here and there as courageous principals, and maverick schools will work successfully against the odds. But the idea is to increase the odds that extraordinary performance and quality schooling will become routine events across America's educational landscape; however, increasing the odds requires active involvement of the school superintendent. The involvement of the superintendent and the central office is particularly crucial for schools that want to secure such ideas as empowerment and site-based management.

In the summer of 1988, for example, the San Diego Unified School District made a commitment to change the role of the central office and to restructure the relationship between the office and each of the 118 schools in the district. Instead of serving as directors, monitors, and enforcers of district policies and rules the central office managers were to become "enablers" and "facilitators." According to *Education Week*,[23] "Superintendent of schools Thomas W. Payzant informed his staff that no one with the exception of himself and the deputy superintendent, could reject an innovative plan proposed by a school." The intent was to change the central office from a command post to a service center. Commenting on the change assistant, superintendent Catherine Hopper notes, "We were the decisionmakers and it was top down decisionmaking, there's no doubt about it. We whip schools into shape with our little agendas and our checkoff lists." Now the central office asks lots of questions and encourages the schools to come to them with problems and proposals. Schools are encouraged to take charge of their own destiny, initiating programs that make sense to them provided that they are consistent with broad district policies. A procedure exists for individual schools to seek waivers from existing policies and rules. Once the green light is given, the enormous resources of the central office are put at the disposal of the school to help ensure its success.

The Principal as "Principal Teacher"

It's fair to ask what the effects of teacher empowerment and other attempts to enhance the professional status of teachers will have on principals. Will the principal's role be diminished or enhanced? The answer will depend on whether a particular principal regards her or himself as the "boss" or as principal teacher. If the principal is viewed as a principal teacher who has broader responsibilities than other teachers, then having better trained and more involved and responsible colleagues to supervise enhances importance and prestige. This is the case in other professions where senior colleagues routinely

assume responsibility for junior ones. Head surgeons, senior law partners, and chief engineers gain in power and prestige as their staffs
become more competent and influential. If the principal is viewed as
boss, having a management position separate from teaching, it results
in ideas such as teacher leadership and empowerment becoming challenges to the boss's authority.

If the principal is viewed as leader of leaders and responsible for
helping teachers, parents and others assume a greater share of responsibility and obligation for what happens in the school, then her
of his role becomes decidedly more "executive" than "managerial."
Executives are concerned with the broad administration of affairs,
ensuring fidelity to agreed-upon values and goals, building commitment and motivating others. Managers are concerned with directing
and monitoring people and events. Managers always work for
executives.

Parents as Partners

Empowerment, enablement, and enhancement need to be expanded
to include parents in the governance and process of schooling. Parents
must be invited to participate. Schools need to help them participate
by removing obstacles and showing them how. If meaningful parent
participation is achieved, the process of schooling improves and this
improvement enhances the roles of principals, teachers, and parents.
Enhanced roles means all three groups will feel better about themselves and have a greater sense of efficacy, conditions that lead to
increased commitment and better results.

There are three overarching reasons why the three E's of value-
added leadership, empowerment, enablement, and enhancement need
to be directed to parents in a manner that allows them to become
partners in school governance and in the education of their children:

- Parents should be involved. It is the right thing to do even
  though at times doing so makes life more complicated for school
  people. *This is the democratic reason.*

- Parents need to be involved. Parent involvement builds commitment and helps in the development of a common and shared
  conception of schooling, enabling children to achieve better and
  learn more. *This is the practical reason.*

• Parent involvement represents the schools' commitment to justice and equity. This commitment is particularly important in our increasingly multicultural society where the background and characteristics of school people are often quite different than those of the parents and children they serve. *This is the moral reason.*

Making the case for parental involvement is easier than finding the right mix of involvement that protects the obligation of the state and the rights of professionals in the process of schooling. Traditionally teachers and other school professionals have assumed the role of experts, relegating parents to the role of client who consumes expert services. This model of low-parent and high-professional control may have worked in a more simple time but just doesn't fit anymore.

Many parents who are unhappy with this traditional view of participation propose a more radical one within which parents are considered to be experts. Teachers and principals are paid consultants who provide advice and services. This high-parent, low-professional control model is impoverished because it compromises the interests of the state in the educational process and underutilizes the talents of professionals.

A more balanced view proposes a partnership within which parents are considered to be expert generalists concerned with all aspects of the welfare of the child; health, recreation, education, moral, social and psychological. Teachers and other professionals (such as guidance counselors, physicians, and ministers) are considered to be expert specialists who decide and provide advice and services. As expert generalists, however, it is the parent who assumes responsibility for coordinating this process. Within this partnership control is high but shared for both parents and school.

Within New York City's Local District No. 4, which encompasses East Harlem, there has been a long history of parental involvement. The district has experimented with providing parents with freedom of choice programs since 1973 and has developed a number of alternative programs in response to parents' needs and wishes. The result has been a 400 percent increase in the number of students who can read at grade level (from 15 to 64 percent) in the last 15 years and the creation of school programs that are so outstanding that they attract students from affluent neighborhoods to East Harlem. Within these high-parent-involvement schools it is clear that parents do not run the schools. It is just as clear that professionals do not enjoy a monopoly either. Both work together as partners with goods results.

According to Stanford University researcher Henry M. Levin, the schools involved in that university's Accelerated Schools Program (designed to accelerate the learning of disadvantaged students so that they are able to perform at grade level by the end of elementary school) owe much of their success to their ability to involve parents as partners. Three major assumptions underlie the Accelerated Schools Program approach: "First, the strategy must enlist a unity of purpose among all the participants. Second, it must 'empower' all of the major participants and raise their feelings of efficacy and responsibility for the outcomes of the school. Third, it must build on the considerable strengths of the participants rather than decrying their weaknesses."

Key in this program is the linking of school and parent empowerment to a common set of goals, values, and purposes that are shared. Empowerment, then, becomes the necessary means by which these purposes become real. Building on strengths recognizes that success will require full utilization of "all the learning resources that students, parents, school staff, and communities can bring to the educational endeavor." Unless the school recognizes and believes that parents have much to contribute, no matter how humble their backgrounds, only the illusion of school partnership will be attained. In Levin's words, "Parents have considerable strengths in serving as positive influences for the education of their children, not the least of which a deep love for their children and a desire for their children to succeed." By the same token "teachers are capable of insights, intuition, and teaching and organizational acumen that are lost in schools that fail to draw upon these strengths by excluding teachers from participating in the decisions that they must implement. Both parents and teachers are largely underutilized sources of talents in the schools."[24]

Philadephia's George Washington School principal, Judy Lechner Knowles, believes that parent involvement is key to effective schooling. When she became principal only two parents were identified with the local Home and School Association. The most common issue which brought parents to school was discipline; rarely were they involved for other reasons. Knowles recognized that, in order for parent participation to increase, the contexts of their participation needed to be reframed. To achieve this reframing she initiated a number of programs including a monthly student recognition day. Parents were sent letters congratulating their child's achievements and inviting them to an awards assembly where their child would be honored. At the assembly a tradition was begun asking parents to stand and receive applause for their role in supporting their children. Knowles worked hard to convince parents that they were an important resource to the school and that teaching and learning would improve if they were more meaningfully involved. She hired as many parents as possible: "One as a School Community Coordinator, two as noon-day aides, one as a reading aide, one as a substitute office aide, two as substitute classroom aides, and a total of 15 were hired with school improvement project funds as parent scholars. These parents found personal satisfaction in coming to the school every day and were paid, although the salaries were minimal." Knowles points out that most of the parents that were employed volunteered time even when they weren't working. They became partners in her efforts to bring about school improvements. Continuing to reframe the context of their participation Knowles included parents on school committees. "One parent who served as the lab assistant, joined the Science Committee. Four other parents joined the School Climate/Discipline Committee and regularly attended the after school meetings." Knowles states "as a result of these interactions . . . credibility was built. Building credibility with adults was based on a recognition of their competence. From this recognition grew respect and trust. This respect and trust was reciprocated."

Enabling leadership needs to accompany efforts to empower parents. Many, particularly minority and poor parents, will need help in learning how to become involved in schooling in an efficacious way. San Diego's Sherman school coprincipals Cecilia Estrada and Dennis Doyle enabled parents by offering parent institute classes designed to help them with things they can do at home that supported school efforts. For example, they taught parents to converse in "educationese" thus enabling them to better understand what teachers were talking about. They initiated programs that encouraged home contacts by school people. Estrada points out that Sherman's Parent Institute Program was developed by the parents themselves to reflect their concerns and interests in learning about the U.S. system. More than 160 parents participated in the six week sessions.[25]

Sherman's commitment to parent involvement spills over into the informal life of the school. Dennis Doyle comments, "We know from the research that most contact with the home .. is negative, particularly for black and Hispanic kids. One thing I've been doing is reading to the kids in their homes once a week. . . . I go to the home with the parents' approval in advance and reread orally chapters that the kids have picked as their favorites. They get to invite a certain number of their friends and neighbors to come and listen. I have had some wonderful readings with a mixture of preschoolers, high schoolers, and grandmothers. We usually have milk and cookies together afterwards. It is fun for all of us but it also helps me learn more about what is happening in the home."[26] By reading to the children coprincipal Doyle is modeling firsthand a supportive learning environment for the home.

The Extended School-Community

Irene Diedrich-Rielly, the principal of Glen Grove School in Glenview, Illinois, believes that school leaders must define their communities differently. She points out that "too often principals identify themselves with the central office or to some combination of central office, the school, and the parents of children in the school." She believes that an extended view of community that involves neighboring businesses and public service organizations provides a more appropriate and effective conception of school-community. Saanichton, British Columbia, Superintendent Janet Mort agrees. Noting that only 20 percent of the adults in the Saanich school district had children in the school and feeling that the kind of school support and commitment needed for excellence could not be realized by this minority, Mort adopted a policy requiring all school-based public relations efforts to be directed at the extended school community.

Principal Diedrich-Rielly's school was located a half-mile from the headquarters of the Zenith Corporation. Zenith frequently used the school grounds for company baseball games and other events. Diedrich-Rielly made it a point to meet Zenith's president and board chairman on the grounds of the playground during one of these events. Conversations with these two persons led to a "school-business partnership that benefited both parties." Research and development personnel from Zenith work with kids in creative aspects of science and sponsor a science fair. Children display their artwork in a corporate art gallery. Zenith employees help with tutoring and other special needs. The school chorus sings for Zenith employees. Zenith-Glen Grove school traditions and rituals began to evolve serving to bond together both school and corporation.

To Diedrich-Rielly the problem was how to bring together two different cultures to serve a common purpose. The shared playground represented a small crack in both cultures that allowed for a new configuration. Her advice, "Look for breaks in a culture and take advantage of these breaks. Routine leadership involves evolutionary change. But sometimes what is needed is more dramatic change. Principals must look for occasions, breaks in the culture, if they seek to make changes that represent significant departures from ordinary ways of doing business."

For Mount Kisco, New York, Elementary School principal John Finch the break in the culture was an opportunity to provide school facilities for a day care and preschool program serving four year olds. In addition to this program the school houses an active Parent Center, an incorporated parent cooperative with its own Board of Directors. Parents volunteer services and pay dues to the center. About 100 families take advantage of the center's programs that include workshops on parenting and parent maintained and managed cooperative playgrounds. The center provides children with a play area, a library and dining area, and comfortable arrangements for parents to visit informally and to engage in workshop activities. Principal Finch points out that there is a partnership with parents as a result of the Parent Center— a partnership characterized by close communications between teachers and parents. In his words, "It is a good example of home and school working together. Schools can't do it alone."[27]

According to *Education Week* the Independence Missouri schools have added a new "tier" to regular school offerings: full-time care for three-to-five year old children of working parents. Care is provided before, during and well after regular school hours. The district also provides parenting classes, home visits to parents of infants from birth to three years, training for day care providers, counselling, health screening and other services.[28] It is clear to school officials in Independence that investments in parents represents an investment in the future successful schooling of their children.

The Saanichton school district has important ties with a number of local businesses including AT&T Canada and the local newspaper. This kind of connection has proved effective not only in building school-community relations but in providing for better teaching and learning. As Superintendent Mort explains, "Four years ago we couldn't get the press to put articles in the newspaper about our schools because they weren't controversial enough. Now the press calls every couple of days to see if there's a new project or some new innovation that they should be paying attention to and should be writing about." Schools looking for happy endings such as these should heed well the advice of Superintendent Mort and Principals Diedrich-Rielly and John Finch—expand one's conception of school community to include the extended community.

The Bottom Line

Harvard University's Rosabeth Moss Kanter, a leading expert on power in organizations, believes that the consequences of not providing people with *opportunity and of not sharing power* are damaging both to them personally and to their organizations. She asserts that people who view their opportunity for personal growth and advancement and for participation as low tend to limit their aspirations, have lower self-esteem, seek satisfactions outside of work, are critical of management, are less likely to seek changes openly preferring to gripe informally and to stir the undercurrent, steer peer groups toward defensiveness and self-protection, emphasize social relationships over tasks, be more parochial, become complacent, and become concerned with survival and economic security rather than intrinsic aspects of job. Persons who view themselves as being low in power tend to encourage and promote low morale, be critical, behave in authoritarian ways over their own charges, seek to gain and retain control, discourage growth and opportunities of subordinates, be more insecure, and protect turf.[29] It's pretty hard to imagine quality schooling emerging from principals, teachers, and parents who harbor these feelings and possess these characteristics.

The value-added leadership rule for building genuine parent partnerships and for bonding together principals, teachers, and parents is simple. *Once purposes are in place and shared values are known, practice a policy of inclusion by promoting the three E's of value-added leadership: empowerment, enablement, and enhancement.* That's the bottom line for quality schooling.

9

Getting Practical: Enhancing Collegiality and Intrinsic Motivation

Collegiality and intrinsic motivation are both powerful and practical school-improvement strategies. They are the value-added leadership dimensions that are necessary to build a professional culture of teaching with standards, norms, and practices aligned to excellence. This chapter demonstrates that building a professional culture of teaching is the only alternative available to us if we seek excellence in a world of schooling that is loosely connected managerially but tightly connected culturally. It is argued that the peculiar combination of looseness and tightness that characterizes schools means that nothing else will work. For this reason value-added leaders consider collegiality and intrinsic motivation to be practical school-improvement strategies.

Despite the importance and practicality of collegiality and intrinsic motivation, the two are sometimes mistrusted and often misunderstood. Policymakers and school administrators, for example, often confuse congeniality with collegiality and extrinsic motivation with intrinsic. Let's first examine collegiality and then turn our attention to intrinsic motivation.

- Congeniality refers to the friendly human relationships that exist among teachers and is characterized by the loyalty, trust, and easy conversation that result in the development of a closely knit social group.

- Collegiality refers to the existence of high levels of collaboration among teachers, and is characterized by mutual respect, shared work values, cooperation, and specific conversation about teaching and learning.

- When congeniality is high, a strong informal culture aligned with social norms emerges in the school. The norms may or may not be aligned with school purposes. Sometimes the norms contribute to and at other times interfere with increased commitment and extraordinary performance.

- When collegiality is high, a strong professional culture held together by shared work norms emerges in the school. The norms are aligned with school purposes, contributing consistently to increased commitment and extraordinary performance.

Congeniality and collegiality are very different. Congeniality refers to friendly human relationships and the development of strong supporting social norms that are *independent* from the standards of the teaching profession and the purposes and work of the school. Collegiality, by contrast, refers to principals and teachers sharing, helping, learning and working together in response to strong supporting work norms that emerge from professional standards and school purposes.

Both congeniality and collegiality are desirable and together comprise value and value-added dimensions of leadership. However, congeniality without collegiality can result in the development of informal norms that may be work-restricting resulting in less effective teaching and learning for students. For example, teachers might informally agree that the price of membership in the social group is to give a "fair day's work for a fair day's pay" but not to exceed this limit. Teachers are expected to do what they are "supposed to," thus avoiding problems with management, but never more. They become oriented to the minimum, not the maximum necessary for quality schooling. New teachers who want to join the group will have to abide by the informal rules of this work-restrictive culture in exchange for accepted membership.

When congeniality is combined with collegiality, work-enhancing values and norms are actually reinforced; but this ideal combination is not necessary for excellence. Many cases exist in both the corporate world and schools where the climate is "strictly businesslike." Shared work norms are strong and people cooperate. They are cordial to each other but are not particularly close socially. Though value-added leaders may enjoy and promote congeniality, their emphasis is on providing the climate and conditions that enhance the norms of collegiality.

Recent research independently reported by University of California, Berkeley professor, Judith Warren Little, and Susan Rosenholtz of the University of Illinois provides compelling support for the importance of collegiality in building a professional culture of teaching on the one hand and in enhancing commitment and performance on the other. Both researchers found that the kind of leadership principals provided influenced the collegial norm structure of the school. Rosenholtz found that teachers in high-collegial schools describe their principals as being supportive and as considering problems to be schoolwide concerns that provided opportunities for collective problem solving and learning. Teachers and principals in less collegial schools, by contrast, reported being isolated and alienated.[1] In her research, Little found that norms of collegiality were developed when principals clearly communicated expectations for teacher cooperation; provided a model for collegiality by working firsthand with teachers in improving the school; rewarded expressions of collegiality among teachers by providing recognition, release time, money, and other support resources; and protected teachers who were willing to buck expected norms of privatism and isolation by engaging in collegial behaviors.[2]

Getting Practical from a Management Perspective

Despite the evidence linking successful schooling with the development of a professional culture of teaching that supports and extends collegiality, many principals and superintendents remain hesitant. They recognize that the more collegiality is emphasized, the less appropriate will be many of the management practices that are now in place in our schools; but promoting collegiality is nothing more than being practical in a management sense. As work gets more complex, as the context of work gets less stable and more dynamic, and as structural looseness becomes more pronounced the only way in which work can be coordinated is through collaboration.

For example, fast-food restaurants, high-tech corporations, schools, and other organized enterprises have in common the need to coordinate different jobs, tasks, and responsibilities to ensure that employees fulfill their responsiblities. Meeting this essential management requirement involves two contradictory strategies: assigning different responsibilities to different persons (what is known in management as *differentiation*) and bringing the work of these same people together to serve a common purpose (*integration*). Coordinating the work of people who have different responsibilities and/or who are located in different places is the way organizations achieve the needed integration. How management chooses to coordinate makes a difference. For an enterprise to function optimally, coordination strategies need to be matched with the degree of work complexity involved. If not, then the work will become simplified to match the coordination strategy, and performance will be negatively affected as a result.

McGill University management expert Henry Mintzberg points out that organizations have available four different coordinating strategies to ensure that responsibilities are met and work is brought together to serve a common purpose: directly and closely supervising workers; standardizing work processes and work output requirements; enhancing and standardizing worker knowledge and skills; and relying on informal mutual adjustment that results from the need to cooperate (collaboration and collegiality).[3]

As the work of the organization changes from simple and straightforward to complicated and dynamic, the coordinating strategy needs to change. Direct supervision and standardizing of both work processes and outcomes are appropriate and effective for organizations having simple work (the factory, the fast-food restaurant) but not for more complex organizations (medical teams, high-tech companies, schools). Enhancing and standardizing the knowledge base and relying on collaboration and collegiality is more appropriate for these more professional work settings. The reasons are practical ones. The loose connectedness of complex organizations does not make it possible to directly supervise what people are doing. Standardizing the work results in work simplification and in a less sophisticated, poorer quality product. For example, under direct and close supervision teachers teach according to the system's recipe; but when alone they teach in ways that make sense to them. When faced with an attempt to standardize their work, teachers resist by giving the appearances of complying.

When teachers are not able to resist close supervision and work standardization any longer, something has to give and invariably the work of teaching changes from situational and complex to simple and routine. This reality is a play on the old adage "form must follow function or function will follow form." Unfortunately, simplifying and routinizing the work of teachers will not provide the quality of schooling needed to serve this country well in tomorrow's increasingly complex world. Given this reality, building and enhancing norms of collegiality and providing the organizational arrangement that encourages collaboration become matters of managerial practicality.

Opportunity and Capacity Are Key

Writing in the award-winning *Men and Women of the Corporation,* Rosabeth Moss Kanter pointed out that direct supervision, standardization practices, and other bureaucratic means of seeking coordination do not control what one does as much as they control what one cannot do. Such practices restrict the range of options available to teachers and principals. Fewer options means that teachers and principals will be less likely to respond to the intellectual challenges and academic demands they face on the one hand and to the unique needs and requirements of students and parents on the other. Everyone loses as a result. Limiting options of teachers and principals is bad educational policy.

As a result of her research Kanter found that "opportunity" and "power" were the essential characteristics necessary for effective performance in complex work. Opportunity refers to the perception teachers and principals have of the future prospects for advancement, increased responsibility, status, prestige and challenging work on the one hand and for increasing knowledge, skills and rewards on the other. Power refers to "the ability to get things done, to mobilize resources, to get and use whatever it is that a person needs for the goals he or she is attempting to meet." Kanter notes that too little opportunity and power results in the rapid decay of whatever interest and excitement exists in one's job.[4]

Stanford University researchers Milbrey Wallin McLaughlin and Sylvia Mei-Ling Yee point out that a collegial school environment enhances both levels of opportunity and capacity (their label for Kanter's power) for teachers, resulting in greater stimulation at work and higher levels of work motivation. They found that a teacher's effectiveness in a classroom, job satisfaction, and professional growth were directly linked to the opportunities they had to develop basic competence; the availability of stimulus and challenge in teaching; feedback about their performance; support for trying new things; and support for their growth. In their words, "Level of opportunity means much more than the availability of weekend workshops or afterschool staff development sessions. Many factors—both informal and formal—comprise important opportunities. Our teachers mentioned . . . attending conferences, participating in informal mentor relationships, sharing ideas with other teachers; observing other classes and being observed. . ."[5] Teachers in their study commented as follows:

> "I'd like more people to come and visit my classroom—to look, visit, comment. Not to visit with an evaluative purpose, but with the purpose of commenting on what's going on in the classroom. I'd really like feedback from my peers."
>
> "I want nonthreatening feedback from someone who has the time to really take a hard look. It would have to be someone whom I respected and looked up to, and they would have to value the same things I do in teaching. I need a comfort zone, a framework around me within which I have the freedom to be myself—to use my own judgment and get trust and respect."
>
> "Coming to this school [with its high level of collegial interaction] had a tremendous impact on my attitude as a teacher. I found the staff as a whole more happy, more excited about teaching, more creative. In turn I became more excited and innovative about my own teaching . . . and less drained at the end of the day."[6]

Opportunity and capacity were the ingredients Seattle's Montlake Elementary School principal Lavaun Dennett provided in building a collegial faculty. Though satisfied with the faculty and believing that Montlake was a good school, she felt that the school was not working to full potential. She spent an entire summer working with the district Director of Special Education and the assistant superintendent coming up with a plan to radically restructure the school in a way that would dramatically reduce class size. This would be accomplished by using all of the teachers in the building to teach a "regular" classroom of students without pullout classes for Special Education (Chapter 1). As Dennett notes, prior to the start of the school year:

> We organized a two day staff workshop and sent the staff an invitation. "How would you like to have class sizes of 20 students? How would you like to see every child in your class successful?" They came. Eager, laughing, incredulous.
>
> After two days of talking about the model and planning next steps, the staff could hardly wait for school to get started. Shortly afterwards, the Seattle Education Association went on a 19-day strike! We talked out the window and on the sidewalk and continued the planning and preparation. We sent wonderful letters to parents telling them what a great year we had planned. We waited. And we waited. Finally the Education Association got an acceptable settlement and we went to work. Never had the work been so exciting. Or so rewarding. In many ways the staff worked harder than ever before. They spent extra hours after school in training and planning sessions, usually without pay. They spent more time communicating with one another and with parents. They created new lessons. They went to workshops and brought back new ideas.

Dennett reports that the change in students was even more dramatic. "Test scores went up dramatically, smiles became more and more contagious. Kids were so successful in classes that they stopped getting referred to Special Education."

In spite of its importance in enhancing both opportunity and capacity for teachers, collegiality does not come easy to Americans. Our culture tends to pride independence, self-reliance and competition over cooperation and interdependence. This tradition does not encourage the building of norms of collegiality around group loyalty and other values of congeniality. Collaboration U.S. style needs to be built around ideas, values, beliefs, and commitments. Americans work together when we share common commitments and purposes and when we believe in the same goals. This commonness of purpose and commitment emerges in part from an established professional culture and in part from purposing provided by value-added leadership.

Purposing can be viewed as a compass that points the direction for a school or as a road map that details the way. In loosely connected schools engaged in complex work the compass view fits better. Harvard Business School Professor, Robert H. Hayes explains: "when you are lost on a highway, a road map is very useful; but when you are lost in a swamp whose topography is constantly changing, a road map is of little help. A simple compass—which indicates the general direction to be taken and allows you to use your own ingenuity in overcoming various difficulties—is much more valuable."[7] When organizations are driven by the "compass" of purpose, collegiality becomes the strategy for achieving the needed coordination. Teachers and principals bonded together in a shared commitment decide what to do in the face of changing events by interacting with each other as colleagues as they work.

Team Leadership Can Help

When he was principal of the Webster school in New Rochelle, New York, Robert J. Stephens was able to enhance both purposing and collegiality by demonstrating a commitment to shared leadership. Ignoring union regulations and personnel office practices he decided to involve teachers in the recruitment and hiring of staff at Webster. He began by asking for volunteers from among the faculty who would serve on a school-based selection committee. Not surprisingly this invitation was met with suspicion. The teachers just didn't believe that Stephens meant what he said in asking for their full participation. He did manage to get three teachers to reluctantly agree to serve.

Suspicion changed to enthusiasm as the process continued. The committee discussed and interviewed candidates, assessing both their competence and their fit with what the school represented. To do the job properly the teachers had to come to grips with what the Webster school stood for and what was meant by proper fit. This resulted in an emerging identity for the school that had a tremendous impact over the next several years. Soon teachers became eager to serve on the selection committee. "They became competent at questioning. They looked for skills and competence. They learn to dismiss certain questions and began to ask more substantive, thought provoking questions which involved situations." Not only were classroom teachers involved in this process but members of the support staff and teacher assistants also participated thus providing a broader base of input into decisions in the building.

Webster became known as a team-based school and "people in the community began to view Webster teachers as a certain breed." Shared leadership, in this case, not only helped Webster come to grips with its basic purposes and commitment but provided a basis for building a sense of collegiality among the staff. As Principal Stephens would put it, "Our teachers think of each other as colleagues not competitors."

Corporate America has discovered anew the importance of the "people factor" in increasing competitiveness. What is different this time is the emphasis on recognizing people as key links to success— indeed as valuable resources for the corporation rather than just treating them "nice" to avoid problems. If you asked General Motors executive vice president Alan Smith what the winning ingredient was for corporate success he would respond:

> Technology? Very important.
>> Capital? You've got to have it, and there's a lot around.
>> Good plants and equipment? They're also important.
>> But it's *people* that will make the difference.[8]

Smith believes that the company must set the climate for people to succeed by demonstrating by deeds as well as words that people are "our most important asset." To him this asset is best invested in excellence through teamwork. Principal Stephens would do very well as a manager at General Motors. By the same token lawmakers, state departments of education, and local school district officials would take a giant step on the road to excellence if their policies followed the lead of Smith and Stephens. Opportunity and capacity, teamwork and collegiality when combined with purposing, leadership by outrage, and other dimensions of value-added leadership are the powerful ideas needed for building a professional culture of teaching aligned with excellence. One such additional dimension of value-added leadership is intrinsic motivation, the topic of the next section.

The Motivation Challenge

Intrinsic motivation plays an important role in value-added leadership. Too often, however, intrinsic motivation is confused with extrinsic, making the practice of this leadership difficult. American managers, for example, have been successful in getting required performance from workers; but the motivation challenge is to get extraordinary performance and on a sustained basis. Getting extraordinary performance from teachers and principals requires throwing away policies and practices that are based on traditional conceptions of motivation. Value-added leaders know that extraordinary commitment and performance over time cannot be bought, cajoled through clever leadership styles, forced by the rules, or achieved by controlling and inspecting. These traditional strategies can get people to do what they are supposed to but not more.

Extrinsic motivation is based upon the value a person receives from the *external* context of the work. Better working conditions, more money, a new title, prizes and awards, and compliments from supervisors are examples of extrinsic motivators. When extrinsically motivated teachers and principals are pushed by external rewards and punishments. "What gets rewarded gets done" is the philosophy. But their connection with the work they do is calculated. Work gets done as long as rewards are provided. When management cannot come up with the rewards desired by workers, they lessen their initiative and downgrade their performance.

Intrinsic motivation, by contrast, is based upon the value received from *the work itself*. Feelings of competence and achievement, excitement and challenge, meaning and significance, enjoyment and moral contentment that one receives from successfully engaging in the work are examples of intrinsic motivators. When intrinsically motivated, teachers and principals are pulled by an inner desire to be effective. "What is rewarding gets done, gets done well, and gets done on a sustained basis." Involvement with work is internal or moral or both.

Yale University professor, Robert J. Sternberg points out that "people who constantly need prodding or rewards or the fear of punishment to get tasks done are extrinsically motivated."[9] They work not because they believe in or enjoy the work but because they have to please others. "The biggest problem with extrinsic motivation is that it disappears when the rewards and punishments do."[10] When teachers are motivated by extrinsic means their involvement with work is calculated. A fair day's work is given for a fair day's pay and this rule is hardly a recipe for excellence in our schools.

The Hazards of Relying on Extrinsic Rewards

What happens when extrinsic rewards are introduced in jobs where teachers and principals are already involved in intrinsically interesting and satisfying work? Is the work enhanced, diminished, or left unaffected by the introduction of these rewards? This is an important policy question because many efforts to improve schools rely on the introduction of extrinsic rewards. Edward L. Deci and Richard M. Ryan, two leading work motivation experts, conclude that the introduction of extrinsic rewards can actually diminish one's intrinsic interest in the work, resulting in reduced commitment and lower performance.[11] A person's involvement with work, for example, changes from internal and/or moral to instrumental and calculated. Work performance becomes dependent upon exchanges and bargains. Whether extrinsic rewards will backfire or not depends on whether teachers and principals view them as *controlling* or *informational*.[12]

Rewards are viewed as controlling if they are intended to get workers to do something that the leader wants. They are viewed as informational if they are viewed as signals and symbols that a person is doing a good job and is appreciated. Throwing a party for a person, handing out buttons for good work, dishing out generous rounds of applause at faculty meetings, sending thank-you notes and so forth all have their place if they are given freely to communicate to teachers and others that they and their contributions are appreciated. The same rewards used to "motivate" a person to do something that the leader wants backfire. For this reason, extrinsic rewards need to be given with no strings attached. Furthermore, nominal extrinsic rewards are likely to work better than substantial ones. Giving a teacher a cash bonus as a sign of "appreciation," for example, is not likely to be viewed as informational but controlling, regardless of intent. The typical teacher asks: "What do I have to do to get it? Now that I have it, what do they want in return?" Too often as a result, intrinsic and moral reasons for work give way to instrumental and calculated ones, with negative results for students in the long run. Extrinsic factors such as money do play an important role in obtaining and maintaining "a fair day's work for a fair day's pay." They are not, however, very good motivators of extraordinary commitment and performance. They can get people to do what they are supposed to but not more, at least not on a sustained basis.

The Secret of Motivation is in the Work Itself

A number of well-known work researchers and management experts have pointed out that the secret to motivating extraordinary commitment and performance over time can only be found in the work itself. Though this understanding is well documented and widely accepted in work-motivation literature and is known to value-added leaders, it is too often ignored in school policies and practices.

Frederick Herzberg, for example, pointed out that such job factors as opportunity for and feelings of achievement and responsibility, interesting and challenging work, and opportunity for advancement have the capacity to motivate.[13] These factors are not something that leaders can give in turn for desired behavior but are an integral part of the work that one does. From their research Richard Hackman and Greg Oldman concluded that enhanced commitment and extraodinary performance were more likely to be present in the following situations:

- When workers found their work to be meaningful, purposeful, sensible, and significant; and when they viewed the work itself as being worthwhile and important.

- When workers had reasonable control over their work activities and were able to exert reasonable influence over work events and circumstances.

- When workers experienced personal responsibility for the work they did and were personally accountable for outcomes.[14]

To Mihaly Csikszentmihalyi enjoyment and "flow experience" are the keys to understanding intrinsic motivation. He studied highly accomplished and motivated experts in a number of different fields (*i.e.*, rock climbers, surgeons, and composers). Though the work of these experts differed considerably each experienced a certain flow that Csikszentmihalyi attributes to intrinsic motivation. Flow is characterized by opportuntiy for action, the merging of action and awareness, focused attention characterized by concentration, narrowing of consciousness and being absorbed in what one is doing, loss of self-consciousness as one works, clarity of goals and norms, direct and immediate feedback, feeling of competence, and being in control of what one does.[15]

Though work psychologists have studied intrinsic motivation in different ways there is a convergence of opinion that the following are characteristics of jobs that enhance intrinsic motivation:

Allow for discovery, exploration, variety and challenge.

Provide high involvement with the task and high identity with the task enabling work to be considered important and significant.

Allow for active participation.

Emphasize agreement with respect to broad purposes and values that bond people together at work.

Permit outcomes within broad purposes to be determined by the worker.

Encourage autonomy and self-determination.

Allow persons to feel like "origins" of their own behavior rather than "pawns" manipulated from the outside.

Encourage feelings of competence and control and enhance feelings of efficacy.[16]

These characteristics must become the criteria for evaluating state mandates, school policies, and management practices if we want to achieve excellence.

Intrinsic Motivation and Student Achievement

Efficacy, intrinsic motivation, and commitment are qualities in teachers that are linked to gains in student achievement. In their sudy of the relationship between teachers' sense of efficacy and student achievement, for example, University of Florida researchers Patricia T. Ashton and Rodman B. Webb found the following when efficacy was high:

Teaching behaviors were characterized by warmth, accepting responses of students, accepting of student initiatives, and attention to students' individual needs.

Student behaviors were characterized by higher levels of enthusiasm and more initiation of interaction with the teacher.

Student achievement was higher in both high school mathematics and language basic skill test scores.[17]

A number of the value-added leadership dimensions discussed in this book that contribute to teachers' sense of efficacy, motivation and commitment are summarized in the figure on page 131.[18]

In few other areas are school leaders and policymakers on firmer grounds when relying on research than in the areas of teacher motivation and collegiality. Furthermore, this research is supported by the compelling realities of practice. Too often, however, policy mandates, administrative directives, and our own comfortable insistence on "business as usual" regarding school management and structure results in conditions and practices that are at odds with what we know is right and effective. As a result, policies and practices encourage bureaucratic teaching, promote isolation, encourage privatism, and discourage cooperation. Decreases in teacher and principal motivation and commitment follow. Bridging the gap between present practice and what we know must be done is the challenge of leadership. If we are to respond to this challenge, collegiality and intrinsic motivation must play key roles in efforts by federal, state, and local authorities to improve our schools.

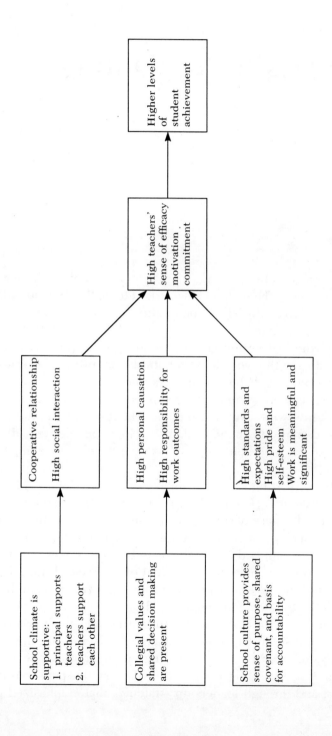

10

Leadership by Outrage

"We feed the children, we transport them to school, we have teachers waiting for them. They don't have a right to do that [not attend]. They don't have a right to fail,"[1] commented Houston superintendent of schools, Joan Raymond, when she mandated that the 40,000 high school students who had failing grades attend special after-school tutoring sessions during the week and on Saturday mornings. Two tutorials a week for every course being failed was the requirement. Furthermore, 1,000 parents were subpoenaed to appear in court to determine why their children were skipping regular school or missing the required tutoring sessions. Raymond explains, "A lot of people are working two to three jobs to pay their property taxes, and we're not going to allow students to waste it."[2]

Wilson Sporting Goods Company chairman, John P. Murray, Jr., and chief executive, Glen N. Rupp, scrapped an entire season's supply of golf clubs because of shoddy workmanship. Some of the clubs were destroyed in the plant's parking lot to communicate to employees a new tone and standard for what was to become a new Wilson.[3]

When Terry Brooks was principal of the Noe Middle School in Louisville, Kentucky, he tried hard to get teachers to abandon traditional methods of teaching reading. They were heavily dependent on the routine use of basal readers, answering questions at the end of the book and so on. He tried to change their view of things by distributing journal articles and providing a number of staff-development opportunities, including University of Louisville-sponsored training sessions, and through leadership strategies that emphasized persuasion. Nothing seemed to work. One day, on the way to a meeting of the language arts department, he decided that he was at the end of his rope and more drastic action was needed. He opened the meeting by burning a basal reader. In his words, "The act was more instinctive than anything else. I wanted the group to know I was serious about trying other approaches to improve the teaching of reading." The group got the message.

The story is often told about Lee Iacocca asking appropriate staff how long it would take for them to bring a convertible to market. The unsatisfactory response was two years. According to the story Iacocca indicated that he "wanted one now" and directed staff to "saw the top off" the existing two-door Chrysler LeBaron model. Convertibles are back quite strongly in today's market as the beautiful newly designed LeBaron and other automobile company entries testify. But Chrysler was able to get the jump on the competition by introducing their earlier "sawed off" version almost overnight and with much success.

After repeated violations, strife and other internal abuses Texas Commissioner of Education William Kirby declared the South San Antonio Board of Education in "default" and appointed a "master" to closely monitor the activities of the board and the school administration with the power to veto any decisions he felt were not in the best interests of the district. Eleven days earlier Kirby lowered the district's accreditation to "warned" status with these words: "I take this action to impress upon the board that we have exhausted all patience and that dramatic improvements must be immediate and sustained."[4] This time his message was ". . . I am warning the board to cease and desist in divisive activities and petty politics and to place its emphasis on working as a team to improve the quality of education in the school district."[5] Improvements in the South San Antonio District were evident within days of this announcement.

Each of these leaders practiced leadership by outrage. Despite standard prescriptions in the management literature that remind leaders to be cool, calculated, and reserved in everything they say or do these leaders brought to their practice a sense of passion and risk that communicated to others that if something is worth believing in then it's worth some passion.

In his extensive studies of successful leaders, Peter Vaill found that their leadership practices were characterized by *time, feeling,* and *focus*. Successful leaders put in extraordinary amounts of time; have very strong feelings about the attainment of the system's purposes; and focus their attention and energies on key issues and variables. The three, Vaill found, are key contributors to building purpose in the enterprise. "Purposing occurs through the investment of large amounts of micro- and macro-Time, through the experience and expression of very strong Feeling about the attainment of purposes and the importance of the system, and through the attainment of understanding of the key variables in system success (Focus). All leaders of high-performing systems have integrated these three factors at a very high level of intensity and clarity."[6] Vaill noted that feeling was the important link between time and focus. His successful leaders cared deeply about the welfare of their particular enterprise, its purposes, structure, conduct, history, future security, and underlying values and commitments. They cared deeply enough to show passion; and when things were not going right this passion often took the form of outrage. Leadership by outrage is a symbolic act that communicates importance and meaning and that touches people in ways not possible when leadership is viewed only as something objective and calculated. Leaders use outrage to highlight issues of purpose defined by the school's shared covenant and this outrage adds value to their leadership practice.

The linking of outrage to purpose is very important. Value-added leaders, for example, know the difference between real toughness and merely looking tough or acting tough. Real toughness does not come from flexing one's muscles, carrying baseball bats, or screaming into bullhorns simply because one happens to have more power than others. Real toughness is always principled. It is value-based. Principals, superintendents, and other school leaders who practice value-added leadership understand that purposing, empowerment, and outrage go together. The three are represented on page 135 in the figure of a target.

The eye of the target represents the core values and beliefs of the school (covenant); the distance between this eye and the outer boundary of the target represents how these values might be articulated and implemented in the practices and work of the school.

Value-added leaders expect adherence to common values but promote wide discretion in how these values are to be implemented. Discretion is promoted by practicing empowerment and enablement. They are outraged when they see these values ignored or violated.

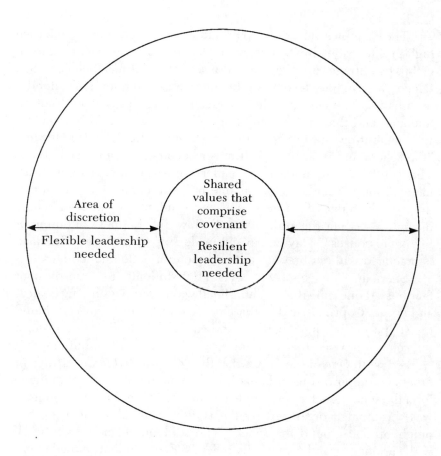

The values of the common core represent nonnegotiables that comprise cultural strands that define a way of life in the school. At the same time teachers, students, custodians, and other members of the school community enjoy wide discretion in organizing their classrooms and work activities, deciding what to teach or do and how, providing that the decisions they make embody the values that are shared and comprise the school's covenant. This is the rule that links purposing with empowerment and enablement and that governs the practice of leadership by outrage: *Everyone is free to do the things that make sense to them providing the decisions they make embody the values that comprise the school's covenant.* When this is not the case teachers, parents, students, and principals have an obligation to be outraged.

The examples of leadership by outrage provided above emphasize high-profile leadership by designated leaders; but the practice of leadership by outrage can take many forms. At the Sherman School in San Diego, for example, leadership by outrage took the form of quiet determination by many people that decline and decay would not be tolerated and the will of many to do something about this situation. In commenting on the Sherman story *Democratic Schools* notes that "the school and its leaders will never become box office sensations. The subtle art of democratic leadership—listening, gaining trust, maintaining wit and wisdom as one helps to organize a community drug watch, grafitti clean-up, or a teacher-student committee on school discipline—is not the stuff that will draw Ted Koppel's attention or fill movie houses."[7] Day in, day out leadership by outrage at Sherman is practiced without bravado but with determination nonetheless.

Sherman is a school with over 1100 students from mostly poor families. At one time the neighborhood was overrun with drug dealers and crime. Coprincipals Cecilia Estrada and Dennis Doyle gathered the support of teachers, parents, and community leaders to transform the school into one that was not only safe and worked, but one that worked well. One of the things that they did was to *kindle outrage in others* by empowering and enabling the community to want to transform the school. As Dennis Doyle comments, "One of our first projects was a campaign organized by the student council to clean up the neighborhood around the school. The students teamed up to work with various city and community officials. Each student council member was paired with an adult as co-captains of a clean-up team. . . . Each team took responsibility for one block. Together they cleaned up 16 blocks adjacent to the school."[8] The students were able to get trash bags from one city agency, a garbage truck from another; they even learned how to operate the truck themselves. They contacted another city agency to get street sweepers into the neighborhood and arrange for tow trucks to haul away burned out and abandoned cars. As the cleaning progressed they put cards in the front doors of all the homes that said "The area in front of your house was cleaned by students at Sherman school."

Doyle notes that vandalism is down 50 to 75 percent over what it was and drug dealers no longer hang out on the street corners. Kids play on the playground after school, and areas where drugs were sold are now used for community gardens. This miracle occurred because of the outrage that Estrada and Doyle were able to kindle in the parents. Two hundred parents got together in a school hosted meeting, and demanded better cooperation from the police. The police responded by bringing in a walking beat and beefing up other enforcement efforts.

In summary, the practice of leadership by outrage can take many forms. Sometimes the practice resembles General Patton in action. At other times Mother Theresa. There is a place for high-profile expressions of leadership by outrage, but when it works best it becomes a shared obligation. Parents, teachers, principals, and students bonded together in a common purpose practice leadership by outrage as needed. Over the long run, therefore, the value-added leader seeks to kindle the potential for outrage in others.

The practice of leadership by outrage needs to become part of educational policy at state as well as local levels if excellence is to be achieved, and this is what is beginning to happen. For example, in a bold expression of leadership by outrage the Council of Chief State School Officers (CCSSO) recently recommended that each of the states enact legislation that guarantees to all students the right to attend a "successful" school.[9] Successful is defined by CCSSO as either a school in which more than 75 percent of the students are performing at or above standard or as a school not at the 75 percent level but improving each year by at least 5 percent. Standards are determined in part by the state and in part by the local school and district and would include such indicators as test scores, other performance indicators (*i.e.*, science displays, musical or artistic exhibits, social studies projects, the number and quality of books read, literary products), dropout rates, participation in extracurricular activities, parent involvement, and student service to the community. Students in schools not meeting at least one of these standards would have the right to transfer to a public school that is up to standard.

This policy represents a statement of "purpose" by the CCSSO. Given the purpose, each individual school in a state would be free to decide for itself what to do and how (empowerment). David W. Hornbeck, who at the time was CCSSO president, stated: ". . . how one achieves the outcomes—which curriculum, what classroom organization, the character of the teaching and administrative force, the length of the school day and year, what textbooks, even where learning occurs (falls within) . . . the decision-making authority of the local schools and school system."[10] States would be responsible for providing assistance to school districts on the one hand and removing bureaucratic obstacles on the other (enabling). In the language of value-added leadership the CCSSO proposes that each school in a state would be free to do the things that make sense to them providing that their decisions embody shared values and purposes. Schools that fall short would be subject to state sanctions and even takeover (leadership by outrage).

Resilient and Flexible Leadership

The practice of leadership by outrage is particularly suited to schools and other enterprises that are loosely connected in a management sense and tightly connected in a cultural sense. This view of tightness and looseness was referred to in chapter 4 as Clockworks II to differentiate it from the Clockworks I view (managerially tight but culturally loose). Unfortunately Clockworks I leaders who practice leadership by outrage are viewed by others as tyrants. The reason for this is that they focus their attention on prescribing and arranging what it is that people will do rather than on the values that guide and nurture the work of the school.

Practicing value-added leadership in Clockworks II schools is more complicated than first seems apparent. It requires the balancing of leadership *flexibility* and *resilience*.[11] Leaders display a great deal of resiliency when concerned with the school's goal structure, values and beliefs, and overall philosophy. At the same time they display a great deal of flexibility when concerned with the everyday articulation of these values in the form of teaching and learning practices and designs.

Before continuing this discussion refer to the Style Flexibility Index and the Style Resiliency Index illustrated on pages 139 and 140. The items comprising these indexes were suggested by the Canadian management expert William J. Reddin.[12] Following the directions provided respond to each of the indexes to obtain your flexibility and resilience scores.

Flexibility in leadership is best understood by comparing it with drifting. Both concepts comprise the same behaviors. Expressing these

Style Flexibility Index

   Think of occasions, situations, and incidents when you as school principal were interacting directly with teachers about *day-to-day* and *week-to-week decisions involving instructional materials, subject-matter content, classroom organization, and the provision of teaching and learning.* As a result of this interaction, indicate how teachers would describe you, using the ten paired statements provided below.

	10 9 8 7 6 5 4 3 2 1	
Other-directed	_____	Dogmatic
Sensitive	_____	Unresponsive
Collaborating	_____	Rejecting
Reality oriented	_____	Status oriented
Interdependent	_____	Authority oriented
Involved	_____	Inhibited
Team player	_____	Uncooperative
Colleague oriented	_____	Control oriented
Open-minded	_____	Close-minded
Practical	_____	Intolerant

10 9 8 7 6 5 4 3 2 1

   Scoring: Sum the scores given to each of the ten scales of the Style Flexibility Index. Scores will range from a low of 10 to a high of 100. The higher the score, the more flexible one is perceived to be. An improved indication of style flexibility would be obtained by having teachers actually describe their principal.

From: T. J. Sergiovanni, *The Principalship A Reflective Practice Perspective.* Boston: Allyn and Bacon, 1987, p. 90.

behaviors in one situation, however, results in effectiveness while in another ineffectiveness. According to Reddin, when the behavior matches the situation the leader will be viewed as being highly flexible by those with whom she or he works. When the same behavior is expressed in inappropriate situations the leader is viewed as drifting. He points out that the flexible leadership style is characterized

Style Resilience Index

Think of occasions, situations, and incidents when you as principal were interacting directly with teachers about *general goals and-purposes, educational platform, and overall philosophy of the school.* As a result of this interaction, indicate how teachers would describe you, using the ten paired statements provided below.

	10 9 8 7 6 5 4 3 2 1	
Clear goals	_____	Inconsistent
Fulfills commitments	_____	Uncommitted
Willpower	_____	Avoids conflict
Individualistic	_____	Conforming
Decisive	_____	Indecisive
Reliable	_____	Disorganized
Self-confident	_____	Avoids rejection
Simplifies issues	_____	Ambiguous
Persistent	_____	Yielding
Tough-minded	_____	Wavering
	10 9 8 7 6 5 4 3 2 1	

Scoring: Sum the scores given to each of the ten scales of the Style Resilience Index. Scores will range from a low of 10 to a high of 100. The higher the score, the more resilient one is perceived to be. An improved indication of style resilience would be obtained by having teachers actually describe their principal.

From: T. J. Sergiovanni, *The Principalship A Reflective Practice Perspective.* Boston: Allyn and Bacon, 1987, p. 89.

by tolerance for high ambiguity, power sensitivity, an open-belief system, and other directedness. Leaders who are flexible in their style are comfortable in unstructured situations but are not control oriented. They display a great deal of interest in the ideas of others and by contrast bring to the work context very few *fixed* ideas of their own.

Flexible leadership characteristics are very desirable when practiced within the loosely structured discretionary space of the school as depicted in the target diagram presented earlier. But when it comes to the school's goal structure and the shared values that comprise its covenant, the characteristics are less desirable and the leader is viewed as drifting. Drifting leadership suggests a lack of direction and an absence of commitment to a purpose or cause.

Reddin suggests the concept of rigidity to help understand counterproductive expressions of resilience. The resilient leadership style is characterized by tough-mindedness, self-confidence, self-discipline, and a strong will. These are qualities that leaders should express when dealing with aspects of the school's value core or covenant; but expressing these qualities when dealing with the day-to-day decisions that teachers make in classrooms results in the leader's being perceived as rigid. The two dimensions of resilience and flexibility can be illustrated in the form of a leadership grid as follows:

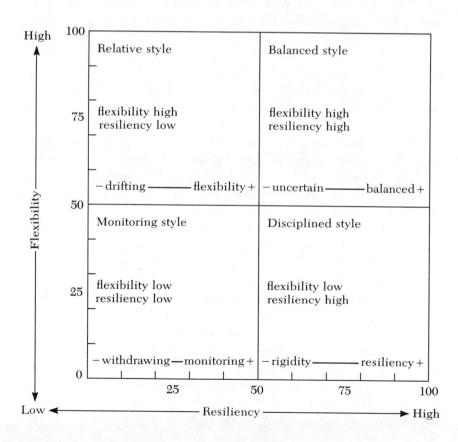

At the base of the grid, resilience scores range from a low of zero to a high of 100. Plot your score from the Style Resilience Index on this dimension. To the left is the flexibility dimension ranging from zero to 100. Plot your Style Flexibility Index score on this dimension. Combining the two dimensions helps us think about the four different styles of leadership: relative, balanced, monitoring, and rigid. Which of the four styles do your scores suggest describes you? Is this an accurate description? If you are not sure, perhaps you might have two or three persons who know you as a leader do the rating for you. Let's examine each of the four styles looking for clues as to how to manage in the Clockworks II world of schooling.

The relative style works best when important values are not at stake and is appropriate for issues that fall into the school's high discretionary area shown in the target diagram. However, when leaders are flexible in dealing with the school's core values they appear to others to be drifting and are not viewed as being able to provide the necessary purposing and direction.

The disciplined style works best for issues related to the school's core of values; but using this style with teachers on issues that deal with the day-to-day activities of schooling is likely to be viewed negatively. The leader, instead of being perceived as resilient, is viewed as being rigid.

The balanced style suggests that the leader be flexible as others work day to day to articulate school goals and purposes. At the same time, the leader provides resilient leadership with respect to the promotion and maintenance of values and purposes. This is the ideal style to which value-added leaders aspire.

The monitoring style comprising both low flexibility and low resilience can work in instances where jobs can be programmed in such detail that the emphasis is less on persons and goals and more on monitoring the work flow, thus ensuring reliability. Prescribing in detail what teachers do, engineering highly specific curriculum-alignment strategies, providing close supervision of the teacher's work, and engaging in other "teacherproof" management strategies are examples of the monitoring style. When used in excess or in inappropriate occasions this style portrays the leader as one who has withdrawn her or his concern for people as individuals and for values and purposes. It is the perfect example of the leader who is preoccupied with *doing things right* and thus neglects *doing right things*.

The Obligation of Democracy

The practice of leadership by outrage acknowledges the importance of freedom and self-sufficiency linked to shared values and norms. This acknowledgement emerges from the understanding of the difference between democracy and anarchy. Democracy provides freedom within a framework of shared values and purposes and always links freedom with obligation. For value-added leaders combining freedom with obligation is the secret to genuine accountability in schools. Anarchy, by contrast, provides freedom without question. Value-added leaders believe that teachers, principals, parents, students, and others involved in the school do not trade in their rights and prerogatives or commitments and responsibilities as members of our citizenry in exchange for school membership. The philosopher Immanuel Kant provides three principles for judging a "good citizenry" and these principles apply as well to all those who live and work together in schools: 1) the freedom of every member of society as a human being; 2) the equality of each with all the others as a subject; (3) the interdependence of each member of a commonwealth as a citizen.[13] Providing freedom, equality, and interdependence within a framework that recognizes individual's rights, common responsibilities and obligations as school members provides the basis for the practice of shared leadership by outrage. Shared leadership by outrage by empowered and enabled "citizens of the school" is a natural expression of the obligation of democracy. It is, indeed, one of the practices associated with moral leadership—the topic of the next chapter.

11

The Corollaries and Some Final Thoughts

The dimensions of value-added leadership and the stages of leadership for school improvement were presented in Chapters 2 and 3. Two corollaries to the dimensions and stages were also provided: build in canvas and emphasize moral leadership. It was pointed out that sometimes value-added leaders need to project an image of the school that helps gain legitimacy or avoid trouble or both. Failure to do so increases the demands and constraints faced thus limiting choices and opportunities to practice value-added leadership. Schools are sponsored by powerful state bureaucracies that force them to operate in bureaucratic ways. Paper must be filed, data accumulated, teachers evaluated according to rule rather than need, schedules followed whether they fit or not, and so on. Further it was noted that these bureaucratic values are sometimes reinforced by rule-happy and top-heavy local school district central offices. If school leaders follow these rules, to-the-letter excellence remains out of reach, and basic competence is endangered. If they do not follow these rules they can find themselves in trouble at the hands of a vindictive bureaucracy.

Faced with the choice of buckling under by complying or "doing a bit of rule bending," successful leaders, whether administrators or teachers, often choose the latter. Xerox Corporation chairman and CEO David T. Kearns and Denis P. Doyle of the Hudson Institute describe them as " 'canny outlaws,' system beaters, creative and responsible rule benders. They have to be to succeed, because in most school districts . . . the deck is stacked against the creative, imaginative and entrepreneurial teachers (and administrators)."[1] In a pioneering study of the characteristics of successful principals, Keith Goldhammer and his colleagues found that they were frequently critical "of the restraints imposed by the central office and of the inadequate resources. They found it difficult to live within the constraints of the bureaucracy; they frequently violated the chain of command, seeking relief for their problems from whatever sources that were potentially useful."[2] Building in canvas is one way to be a successful canny outlaw. The idea isn't to confront the bureaucracy for its own sake but rather to "work the bureaucracy" in an effort to increase the choices that better serve teachers and students. Start with the spirit of the rule—bending it to shape best practice. If the system tightens up, go to the letter of the rule and efficiently do what is necessary with as little energy possible and in a way that minimizes impact.

Fortunately, practicing value-added leadership does not always require major restructuring of the way in which schools are organized. What is required is a change in the way of life or culture of the school. For example, though collegiality flourishes more easily in schools organized as interdisciplinary teaching teams, it can be expressed as well within traditional organizational patterns. Granted, a little more effort from teachers and the principal may be required. The principal may have to juggle the schedule some, or cover a class or two, or otherwise find some extra time to enable teachers to get together for planning, sharing, and helping. Teachers may have to do a little sacrificing as well, but if collegiality is included in the school's shared values everyone will find ways to overcome the traditional egg crate and graded school structure. Empowerment can be expressed similarly. Though empowerment may take the form of a new school governance structure complete with committees and spelled out decision-making procedures, it can flourish as well (and maybe better) as a value that is expressed in the everyday lives of teachers and the principal as they work together.

Bending rules, creating illusions, and building in canvas can raise moral questions. Some critics might charge that many of these ideas are deceptive and have no place in the lexicon of administration. Principals and superintendents who practice value-added leadership, however, believe that moral questions are not raised by being sensitive to the bureaucratic realities of the real world. Instead they would argue that moral questions are raised when these realities are ignored in pursuit of a Don Quixote strategy of change *or* when one buckles under by merely doing things right without regard to doing right things. For value-added leadership to work one needs to make tough choices— choices with important moral consequences for the school. Peter Block believes that the choices must be between:

- maintenance and greatness

- caution and courage

- dependency and autonomy

- approval and integrity[3]

The choice for maintenance, caution, and dependency is the choice to be led by others. This is the easy choice because bureaucratic policies and procedures provide us with a source of security, an easy way out, and the kind of organizational insulation that keeps us from being responsible for what happens. In Block's words, "It is comforting to be led. It feels safe and implies a promise that if we follow, our future will be assured. The choice for dependency is a step into the mainstream along a conventional path."[4] Of course it makes political sense to choose on behalf of maintenance, caution, dependency, and approval from time to time. But when these tactics become the basis of our overarching strategy we forsake excellence for the bureaucratic mentality. The consequences for us, our schools, and the children that are served are serious enough to raise moral issues and ethical questions.

Sometimes choosing what is right by following the dictates of the school's shared values and purposes can get teachers and principals in trouble. This was what happened when Principal Lavaun Dennet and teachers at the Montlake school in Seattle decided to redesign the schedule of their school.[5] Not satisfied with the progress they were making in teaching the basic subjects, they decided that all students should spend the morning on reading and mathematics. Further, the librarian, the science teacher, the special education teacher, and the Chapter 1 teacher were all assigned to teach these subjects, thus allowing for a reduction in class size to about 15 students. During basic skills instruction the students would be grouped by skills rather than by grade level. In the afternoon students would return to the regular schedule for social studies, science, and other school subjects. According to *Education Week* the results were dramatic: "Because teachers shared students during the day, they felt more responsible for the total school and worked more cooperatively. Morale improved. Discipline problems declined. And test scores shot up."[6] Unfortunately this action by the Montlake faculty was in violation of federal Chapter 1 regulations. Special education students, for example, were no longer being labeled. Once the labeling stopped the federal government withdrew its entitlement money and the school lost approximately $100,000 in additional funding.

Though the state and the city school district provided additional money to make up for this shortfall, the support was uneven and unreliable forcing the school to seek additional funding from local corporations and other private sources. At this writing the verdict is still out on Montlake's future since new sources of revenue have not been guaranteed. It would have been easier for Principal Dennet and the Montlake faculty to have conducted business as usual rather than reorganizing in a way that they thought would serve students better. Their funding would have been guaranteed, and they would have had fewer headaches. But they chose otherwise because morally they believed that it was the right thing to do.

The Importance of Faith in Building School Character

An underlying theme in value-added leadership is the importance of exchanging bureaucratic authority for moral authority. The metaphor character can help us to think about "organizational morality" much as we do individual morality. Building and enhancing the school's character is the key to establishing its credibility both internally among students, teachers, parents, and administrators; and externally in the broader community. Brigham Young University professor and management consultant Alan L. Wilkins notes that the components of an organization's character are its common understanding of *purpose* and identity that provides a sense of "who we are"; *faith* of members in the fairness of the leadership and in the ability of the organization, self, and others to get the job done; and, the *distinctive cultural at-*

tributes that define the tacit customs, networks of individuals and accepted ways of working together and with "clients."[7] In his words, purpose, faith and cultural attributes "add up to the collective organizational competence."[8] For Wilkins, faith is a particularly important component of organizational character. Loss of faith in the leadership, in self or the organization, results in loss of character. Building faith restores character. Enhancing faith increases character. Without faith and character the organization and its members are not able to move beyond the ordinary to the extraordinary performance. With faith and character such a transformation is possible.

Along with school culture expert Terry Deal, Wilkins believes that the key to maintaining and enhancing existing faith or restoring lost faith is the ability of the school's leadership to remember and honor the past and to draw upon this past when moving forward to new initiatives. Destroying the past is risky because it casts aside previous investments of competence and hard work of present members. This can result in a loss of confidence in the leadership, a feeling that one's present contributions are not valued, and ultimately a decline in one's perceived self worth.

Among Wilkins's suggestions for remembering and honoring the past are:

- Return to the past for inspiration, insight, and guidance as one moves forward.

- Where the past is an unhappy one attributed to the leadership (for example, a tradition of authoritarian management) "repent" by admitting past mistakes and "reform" by seeking to renegotiate existing relationships with openness and in good faith.

- Identify and highlight the values from the past that will be maintained and the principles and practices that will remain constant.

- Highlight examples among current practices that represent successes to be honored and maintained.

- Enhance the leadership roles (by promotion and other means) of individuals presently on board who can serve as positive examples and models of the new way but are valued for their contributions to the old ways. As Wilkins puts it, "Promote hybrids."

- Study the history of the school and label the eras much as is done in a typical history course. Labeling past eras (i.e., the age of accountability; the nice guy era of John Jones; the years of teacher militancy) allows for labeling of the upcoming era without a loss of continuity or an abandonment of past efforts and achievements. Labeling also helps identify past mistakes and makes it easy to move beyond them.

- Mourn the loss of cherished ideas, values, and practices from the past. Terry Deal, for example, recommends that the cherished past be acknowledged in formal "mourning events" such as ceremonies that celebrate the past but still make clear that it is now time to move on.[11] A high school, for example, that once provided a smorgasbord of curriculum in an effort to be comprehensive but now seeks to emphasize a common core in the tradition of the liberal arts might hold a weeklong celebration highlighting previous achievements of its vocational education curriculum and other educational programs constantly pointing out, nonetheless, the new road to be followed.

Honoring the past is important for maintaining faith in the organization itself and for building moral authority for new initiatives—but not important enough. Faith is maintained or lost by the everyday practices of the school's leadership. The key, according to Wilkins, is whether leaders are viewed as credible in their dealings with others. Do they reward what should be rewarded? Do they reward equitably? Do they express outrage when standards are let down? Do they express outrage fairly? Do they keep their word? Do they explain their actions? Are they reliable? Do they admit their mistakes? In sum, do they practice leadership with integrity? The battle for maintaining and enhancing faith cannot be won in our schools until bureaucratic authority is exchanged for moral.

Leadership by Banking

In collecting the memorable leadership incidents for this book I was struck by a letter from David T. Conley, the Executive Director of

Educational Services for the Poudre Colorado Schools. He provided a critical incident that pointed out the importance of leader modeling values and principles; thus, through example, he pointed the way to needed practices. In the note appended to his incident, Conley provided some insights into the ordinary life of leadership. "I've been struck by the degree to which the better part of leadership is actually 'followership.' In my critical incident I was actually able to provide some relatively unadulterated leadership. But most of what I do has a mixture of leadership and followership: I interpret policies, implement programs, shape and structure behaviors within an organizational framework that is already fairly clearly defined." He added, "I say this only because there is a tendency to focus on the idealistic dimensions of leadership, such as charisma or vision, at the expense of the more mundane but equally important components, such as knowledge of the organization, micropolitics and the elusive concept, timing." His comments point out the danger of substituting the image of leader as *messiah* for that of leader as boss. When we do this, the antidote for bureaucratic management becomes the poison.

The role of messiah unduly links the practice of leadership with personality. It results in connecting too tightly everything that goes on in the school to the personality of the leader: As goes the leader, so goes the school. Obviously leader personality has an important role to play in rebuilding the school culture and in moving forward on the road to excellence. But, in the long run, the leader must be successful in institutionalizing changes by creating a culture of excellence linked to shared purposes, and by providing the needed management support. Personality must give way to purpose and management. When this occurs, the leader is neither boss nor messiah, but administrator.

- The authority vested in leader as *boss* is organizational and hierarchical.

- The authority vested in leader as *messiah* is charismatic and interpersonal.

- The authority vested in leader as *administrator* is obligatory, stemming from the obligation that comes from serving shared values and purposes.

Thus key to value-added leadership is to avoid the mantle of the messiah. This is not easy to do, for being the messiah can be flattering and tempting for a principal. The consequence is that too often school improvements disappear when the leader disappears. Over the long run parents, teachers, and students become too dependent upon the designated leader.

Avoiding the mantle of messiah is a worry for Ruby Cremaschi-Schwimmer, principal of the Lincoln High School in San Diego, California. Prior to her arrival, Lincoln was near the bottom of the heap among high schools in San Diego. The building was in disrepair and students scored low on district tests of reading, mathematics, and language. The school's dropout rates were among the highest. Today Lincoln is a school that works and works well. Much of the credit for its success goes to its principal, who saw her job as a "sacred mission." She was, in many respects, the "messiah" who transformed Lincoln. In her words, "My fears about this 'Guru' approach are that when everything rests on the personality of one individual there is the danger of things regressing when he or she must move on and that too much power residing in one individual leader may lead to the 'Jim Jones' syndrome of leadership with negative results."[12] In her view, leadership must be driven by ideas and obligation—not personality. She is now at work trying to shift the emphasis from what "Principal Cremaschi-Schwimmer believes in and wants" to what Lincoln High School believes in, stands for, and can be. For Lincoln's success to become real, leadership-by-banking must become real.

In his book *Servant Leadership*, Robert K. Greenleaf tells the story of the 18th century American Quaker John Woolman, who almost singlehandedly convinced the society to renounce slavery. He didn't accomplish this by raising a big storm or by the force of charismatic personality. "His method was one of gentle but clear and persistent persuasion. . . . The burden of his approach was to raise questions: What does the owning of slaves do to you as a moral person? What kind of institution are you binding over to your children? Man by man, inch by inch, by persistently returning and revisiting and pressing his gentle arguments over a period of 30 years, the scourge of slavery was eliminated from this society, the first religious group in America formally to renounce and forbid slavery among its members."[13] The concept of servant leadership is popular among Catholic school educators, with Jesus cited as the authority: "You know that rulers of the Gentiles lord it over them and their great men exercise authority over them. It shall not be so among you, but whoever would be great among you must be your servant" (Matthew 20:25).

Servant leadership describes well what it means to be administrator. School administrators are responsible for "ministering" to the needs of the schools they serve. The needs are defined by the shared values and purposes that comprise school covenants. They administer by furnishing help and being of service to parents, teachers, and students. They minister by highlighting and protecting the values of the school. The school leader as minister is one who is devoted to a cause, mission, or set of ideas and accepts the duty and obligation to serve this cause.

Steve Johnson, the principal of the Mark Twain middle school in San Antonio, understands well the ministerial role of school leadership.[14] When Johnson became principal in September of 1987 Twain had a reputation of drug dealing, high absenteeism, low test scores, and tough gang fights. It was considered by many to be "the pits" for both students and teachers. Twain is now a school well on the way to excellence. One would be hard-pressed, however, to have Steve Johnson or assistant principal Kristen Casey take credit for Twain's successes. One rarely sees them either holding the flag up or leading-the-way as would a general lead an army. But they are there every day providing leadership in hundreds of small ways. "Steve Johnson is a good principal. He's not interested in his professional career. Everything he does revolves around what is best for the classrooms, students, and teachers," remarks one teacher. Both Johnson and Casey take turns pulling playground and lunch duty. Johnson assumes responsibility for advising students just like all the teachers do. Casey occasionally teaches a class covering for a teacher in need. Johnson remarks, "This is a good school. There are wonderful things going on here, and I don't think I did anything to cause them to happen. I just want people to be able to teach." Harvard University's Roland Barth points out that "the best principals are not heroes; they are hero-makers."[15] Johnson and Casey prove him right.

Understanding value-added leadership requires that one understand what it takes to be a good follower and what the difference is between being a follower and being a subordinate. For example, followers manage themselves well by thinking for themselves, exercising self control, accepting responsibility and obligation, and believing in and caring about what they are doing.[16] By contrast, subordinates do what they are supposed to, but little else. Typically they want to know specifically what is expected of them. With proper monitoring and supervision they will perform accordingly. They are dependent upon their leaders to provide them with goals and objectives and the proper ways and means to achieve them. They want to know the rules of the game and will play the game as required. Followers are commited people. They are committed to something—perhaps a set of purposes, a cause, a vision of what the school is and can become, a set of beliefs about what teaching and learning should be, a set of values and standards to which they adhere. They need a conviction. Simply put, subordinates respond to authority but followers respond to ideas.

The concept of followership proposes a number of paradoxes.[17] It turns out that effective following is really the same as leadership. Both followers and leaders are attracted to and compelled by the same thing: ideas, values, and commitments. Thus over the long haul value-added leadership seeks to restructure the chain of command so that followers are not connected to leaders in a hierarchical sense, but that both leaders and followers respond to the same ideas, values, and commitments.

Traditional chain of command (hierarchical authority)	Value-added chain of command (moral authority)
Leaders ↓ Followers	Ideas, values, commitments ↓ Leaders as followers and followers as leaders

Value-added leadership is not hard to understand. There are no mysteries to its concepts and ideas. Thus almost any principal or teacher can practice value-added leadership—though it often won't be easy. However the moral stakes are too high for any course of action other than persistence.

Important to the practice of value-added leadership is the ability of leaders to change the content of our schools' "silent language" from bureaucratic to moral. Bill Hampton, the principal of Florissant, Missouri's McCluer North High School, points the way as follows:

> A school isn't only a building, it's an expression of beliefs and attitudes about ourselves and the generation of young people for whom it is planned. In its silent language of space, scale and shape, the structure stands for what we are, what we think of ourselves and what we believe we can become. Whether we are planning programs or buildings, we cannot afford to guide our decisions on anything less than our deepest faith in people.[18]

References

Chapter 1

1. David T. Kearns and Denis P. Doyle, *Winning the Brain Race: A Bold Plan to Make Our Schools Competitive* (San Francisco: Institute for Contemporary Studies, 1988), p. 8.

2. *Ibid.*, p. 9.

3. Thomas W. Payzant, comments prepared for the Holmes Group Seminar on Models of Teaching and Learning. (Michigan State University, July 15, 1988).

4. Christopher Lasch, *The Culture of Narcissism: American Life in an Age of Diminishing Expectations* (New York: W. W. Norton & Co., 1979).

5. Phillip A. Cusick, *The Egalitarian Ideal in the American High School: Studies of Three Schools* (New York: Longman, Inc., 1983). p. 56.

6. *Ibid.*, p. 39.

7. Theodore Sizer, *Horace's Compromise: The Dilemmas of the American High School* (Boston: Houghton Mifflin, 1984), p. 156.

8. *Education Week* (June 22, 1988), p. 17.

9. Peggy Lukens, "Probing 'Myths' About Japanese Education." *Education Week* (November 9, 1988), p. 32.

10. Benjamin Duke, *The Japanese School: Lessons for Industrial America* (New York: Praeger, 1986).

11. *Ibid.*, p. 173.

12. Esther H. Lindsey, Virginia Homes, and Morgan W. McCall, Jr., *Key Events in Executives' Lives.* Technical Report No. 32 (Center for Creative Leadership, Greensboro, N.C., 1987), p. 237.

13. *An Imperiled Generation: Saving Urban Schools.* A report of the Carnegie Foundation for the Advancement of Teaching, (1988), p. 37–38.

14. William W. Purkey, Address to the School Management Assembly, (Trinity University, San Antonio, Texas, August 12, 1987).

15. Harold L. Hodgkinson, *All One System: Demographics of Education— Kindergarten Through Graduate School.* (Washington, D.C.: Institute for Educational Leadership, 1987), p. 18.

Chapter 2

1. Perhaps the five best-known books describing leadership and life in successful corporations and schools respectively are Terrence E. Deal and Alan A. Kennedy, *Corporate Cultures* (Reading, Mass: Addison-Wesley, 1982); Thomas J. Peters and Robert H. Waterman, Jr., *In Search of Excellence* (New York: Harper and Row, 1982); Warren Bennis and Burt Nanus, *Leaders: The Strategies for Taking Charge* (New York: Harper and Row, 1985); Sarah Lightfoot, *The Good High School.* (New York: Basic Books, 1983); and Joan Lipsitz, *Successful Schools for Young Adolescents* (New Brunswick, N.J.: Transaction Press, 1984).

2. H. Ross Perot quoted in the *San Antonio Light* (March 11, 1988). p. B1.

3. James M. Kouzes and Barry Z. Posner, *The Leadership Challenge* (San Francisco: Jossey-Bass, Inc., 1987) p. xv.

4. Colin Moyles's interview notes. Institute of Educational Leadership. Geelong, Victoria, Australia (Undated).

5. Thomas J. Peters and Robert H. Waterman, Jr., *In Search of Excellence: Lessons from America's Best-Run Companies* (New York: Harper and Row, 1982), p. 26.

6. David T. Kearns, "A Business Perspective in American Schooling." *Education Week* (April 20, 1988), p. 24.

7. Susanne K. Langer, *Philosophy in a New Key: A Study of Symbolism of Reason, Rite, and Art* (Cambridge: Harvard University Press, 1978), p. 28.

8. James B. Quinn, "Formulating Strategy One Step at a Time." *Journal of Business Strategy* (Winter 1981), p. 59.

9. Thomas B. Greenfield "Leaders and Schools: Wilfulness and Non-natural Order in Organizations." Thomas J. Sergiovanni and John E. Corbally., eds., *Leadership and Organizational Culture* (Urbana: University of Illinois Press, 1984), pp. 142–169.

10. Warren Bennis, "Transformative Power and Leadership," Sergiovanni and Corbally, *op.cit.*, p. 66. This theme is elaborated in his landmark book written with Burt Nanus, *Leaders: The Strategies for Taking Charge.* (New York: Harper and Row, 1985).

11. *What Next? More Leverage for Teachers.* Joslyn Green, ed. Education Commission of the States, 1986).

12. *A Nation Prepared Teachers for the 21st Century.* Carnegie Forum on Education and the Economy (New York: Carnegie Corporation, 1986).

13. *Time for Results: The Governors' 1991 Report on Education.* National Governors' Report (Washington, D.C., 1986).

14. *Teachers Speak: Quality Schooling for Texas Today and Tomorrow.* Brackenridge Forum for the Enhancement of Teaching (Trinity University, San Antonio, 1987).

15. Arthur E. Wise, *Legislated Learning: The Bureaucratization of the American Classroom* (Berkeley. University of California Press, 1979).

16. Andrew Halpin, *Theory and Research in Administration* (New York: Macmillan, 1967), pp. 131–249.

17. Roland Barth, "The Principal and the Profession of Teaching," Thomas J. Sergiovanni and John H. Moore., eds., *Schooling for Tomorrow: Directing Reforms to Issues that Count,* (Boston: Allyn & Bacon, 1988), p. 230.

18. Judith W. Little, "School Success and Staff Development in Urban Desegregated Schools." (Boulder, Colo: Center for Action Research, 1981).

19. Joan Lipsitz, *Successful Schools for Young Adolescents* (New Brunswick, N.J.: Transaction Books, 1984), p. 35.

20. Peter B. Vaill, "The Purposing of High-Performing Systems" Sergiovanni and Corbally, *op.cit.*, pp. 93–99.

21. Donald M. Kendall, "The Four Simple Truths of Management." *Vital Speeches* (May 15, 1986), as quoted by Albert Shanker, "Where Do We Stand?" *Education Week* (February 17, 1988), p. 11.

22. James G. March, "Administrative Theory and Administrative Life" Thomas J. Sergiovanni and John E. Corbally. eds., *op.cit.*, p. 19.

Chapter 3

1. James MacGregor Burns, *Leadership* (New York: Harper and Row, 1978).

2. Thomas J. Peters and Robert H. Waterman, Jr., *In Search of Excellence: Lessons from America's Best-Run Companies,* (New York: Harper and Row, 1982).

3. Warren Bennis and Burt Nanus, *Leaders: The Strategies for Taking Charge.* (New York: Harper and Row, 1985).

4. Burns, *op.cit.*, p. 20.

5. In his important book, Robert E. Quinn proposes a similar four stage cycle (initialization, uncertainty, transformation and routinization) to describe how a person or group achieves excellence or peak experience. Robert E. Quinn *Beyond Rational Management,* (San Francisco: Jossey–Bass, 1988). pp. 15–23.

6. The story of Principal Kendrick and the Henry W. Eggers Middle School, Hammond, Indiana, including all quotes, is drawn from: Jane A. Kendrick, "The Emergence of Transformational Leadership Practice in a School Improvement Effort: A Reflective Study." Doctoral Dissertation (University of Illinois, Urbana-Champaign, 1987). © Copyright by Jane Kendrick. Used with permission.

7. The standard test scores: Note that the use of three different test batteries during the period 1977–1986 and the addition of 215 transferred students in 1982 make precise comparisons from year to year difficult. Nonetheless the data, when viewed as an indication of a general trend, provide compelling evidence of an upturn in achievement over the period.

Chapter 4

1. Rosemary Stewart, "The Relevance of Some Studies of Managerial Work and Behavior to Leadership Research." James G. Hunt, Uma Sekaran, and Chester A. Schrlesheim, eds., *Leadership Beyond Establishment Views* (Carbondale: Southern Illinois University Press, 1982).

2. "Teachers vs. Curriculum in Philadelphia?" *Education Week,* vol. 7, no. 26 (March 23, 1988).

3. *Ibid.*

4. Karl E. Weick, "Educational Organization as Loosely Coupled Systems," *Administrative Science Quarterly,* vol. 21, (March 1976).

5. James G. March and Johan P. Olsen, *Ambiguity and Choice in Organizations* (Bergan, Norway: Universitetstorlaget, 1976).

6. Karl E. Weick, "Administering Education in Loosely Coupled Schools." *Phi Delta Kappan,* vol. 27 (1982) p. 675.

7. James G. March, "How We Talk and How We Act: Administrative Theory and Administrative Life." in T. J. Sergiovanni and J. E. Corbally, eds., *Leadership and Organizational Culture* (Urbana: University of Illinois Press, 1984), p. 32.

8. "Texas Teacher Appraisal System," *Teacher Orientation Manual* (Texas Education Agency, 1986–87), p. i.

9. Lee Shulman, "Teaching Alone, Learning Together: Needed Agendas for the New Reforms," T. J. Sergiovanni and John H. Moore, eds., *Schooling for Tomorrow: Directing Reforms to Issues that Count* (Boston: Allyn and Bacon, 1989), p. 171.

10. Robert H. Hayes, "Strategic Planning—forward in reverse?" *Harvard Business Review.* (Nov–Dec. 1985), p. 118.

11. William Brown, "Japanese Management. The Cultural Background." *Monumenta Nipponica,* vol. 21 (1966), p. 59.

12. Frederick Herzberg, *Work and the Nature of Man* (New York: The World Publishing Co., 1966).

13. James MacGregor Burns, *Leadership* (New York: Harper & Row, 1978).

14. Bernard M. Bass, *Leadership and Performance Beyond Expectations.* (New York: The Free Press, 1985).

Chapter 5

1. Doron P. Levin, "G. M. Bid to Rejuvenate Leadership." *The New York Times,* (Sept. 3, 1988).

2. Chester Barnard, *The Function of the Executive* (Cambridge: Harvard University Press, 1958. p. 87).

3. Peter Vaill, "The Purposing of High Performance Systems" Thomas J. Sergiovanni and John E. Corbally, eds., *Leadership and Organizational Culture* (Urbana: University of Illinois Press, 1984), p. 91.

4. *Ibid.* p. 86.

5. William J. Bennett, *American Education: Making it Work.* A Report to the President and the American People (Washington, D.C.: Department of Education, April 1988).

6. Joan Lipsitz, *Successful Schools for Young Adolescents* (New Brunswick, N.J.: Transaction Press 1984), pp. 171–174.

7. Warren Bennis, Tranformative Power and Leadership" Sergiovanni and Corbally, *op.cit.*, p. 66.

8. Tom Peters and Nancy Austin, *A Passion for Excellence* (New York: Random House, 1985), p. 286.

9. Robert H. Hayes, "Strategic Planning—forward in reverse?" *Harvard Business Review* (Nov.–Dec. 1985).

10. Doron Levin, "G. M. Bid to Rejuvenate Leadership." *The New York Times* (Sept. 3, 1988).

11. Jay Featherstone, comments to the seminar "Tomorrow's Schools Models of Learning, Models of Schooling." Michigan State University (July 16, 1988).

12. *Principal Selection Guide.* (Washington, D.C.: Department of Education, 1987), p. 5.

13. Lynn Olson, "Children Flourish Here 8 Teachers and a Theory Changed a School World," *Education Week* (Jan. 27, 1988).

14. *Ibid.*

15. Jim Beaty, "Creating an Inviting School Climate: A Principal's Perspective." *Principals Exchange.* Westchester Principals' Center, vol. 3, no. 2 (1988).

16. Peter Block, *The Empowered Manager: Positive Political Skills at Work* (San Francisco: Jossey-Bass, 1987).

17. *Ibid.* pp. 109–121.

18. Thomas J. Peters and Robert H. Waterman, Jr., *In Search of Excellence.* (New York: Harper and Row, 1982).

19. Peter Block, *op.cit.* p. 111–112.

20. *Ibid.*

21. Tom Rusk Vickery "Learning from an Outcomes-Driven School District."
Educational Leadership, vol. 45, no. 5 (1988), pp. 52–56.

Chapter 6

1. Michael E. Porter, *Competitive Advantage: Creating and Sustaining Superior Performance.* (New York: The Free Press, 1985), p. 8.

2. "Discover Daybridge." Daybridge Learning Center. An ARA Services Company.
Note that Daybridge merged with Children's World in 1987 and now operates under
the name Children's World Learning Centers, an ARA Services Company.

Chapter 7

1. The "Meyer story" is summarized from Pamela C. Stanfield and James E. Waller,
"The Principal as White Knight." Paper presented to the American Educational
Research Association (Washington, D.C., 1987). The researchers reached an
agreement with the school district to maintain confidentiality. Thus the name, Meyer,
is a pseudonym and the names Garvin School and Garrett School District are
fictitious.

2. "How Do You Make Your School an Inviting Place?" *Principals Exchange.* vol.
3, no. 2, Westchester Principals' Center, (1988), p. 6.

3. *Ibid.*

4. Ray C. Hackman, *The Motivated Working Adult* (New York: American
Management Association, 1969), p. 158.

5. Terrence E. Deal and Allan A. Kennedy, *Corporate Cultures.* (Reading, Mass:
Addison-Wesley 1982).

6. Terrence E. Deal, "The Symbolism of Effective Schools." *The Elementary
School Journal.* vol. 85, no. 5 (1985), p. 615.

7. *Ibid.,* p. 616.

8. James G. March, "How We Talk and How We Act: Administrative Theory and
Organizational Life" Thomas J. Sergiovanni and John E. Corbally, eds., *Leadership
and Organizational Culture* (Urbana: University of Illinois Press, 1984), p. 31.

9. Deal, *op.cit.,* p. 616.

10. John Saphier and Matthew King, "Good Seeds Grow in Strong Cultures." *Educational Leadership.* vol. 42, no. 6 (1985), p. 72.

11. March, *op.cit.*, p. 32.

12. Robert J. Starratt, "A Theory of Leadership." Undated manuscript.

13. *Ibid.*

14. Edward Pajek, "A Dramaturgical Model of District-Wide Change: The Many Faces of Instructional Supervision." Annual Meeting of the American Educational Research Association, (Washington, D.C., 1987).

15. Georges Polti, *The Thirty-Six Dramatic Situations* (Franklin, Ohio: James Knapp Reeve, 1924), p. 67.

16. Pajek, *op.cit.* p. 11.

17. Polti, *op.cit.* p. 67.

18. A. Paul Hare, *Social Interaction as Drama* (Beverly Hills, CA: Sage Publications, 1985).

Chapter 8

1. Kathleen Devaney and Gary Sykes, "Making the Case for Professionalism." Ann Lieberman, ed., *Building a Professional Culture in Schools* (New York: Teachers College Press, 1988).

2. Gerald Grant, *The World We Created at Hamilton High* (Lilleton, Mass.: Harvard University Press, 1988).

3. Jean Slattery, comments to the Brackenridge Forum for the Enhancement of Teaching. Trinity University, San Antonio (October 18, 1988).

4. *Exxon News* (March 1988).

5. Richard D. Miller, "The Luby Lecture." School Management Assembly, Trinity University, San Antonio (August 12, 1988).

6. David J. Keagans, "A Business Perspective on American Schooling." *Education Week*, April 20, 1988, p. 24.

7. Edward B. Fiske, "Lessons: Are Private Schools Better Because They Have Fewer Administrators?" *The New York Times*, August 31, 1988).

8. *Ibid.*

9. "Not Power but Empower." *Forbes,* vol. 141, no. 12 (May 30, 1988), p. 122.

10. *Ibid.*

11. *Ibid.*

12. *Ibid.,* p. 123.

13. Greg Smith, "Goodyear Workers are Doing Just Fine Without the Bosses." *San Antonio Light,* (September 11, 1988).

14. *Ibid.*

15. Thomas J. Peters, "Quick-fix Incentives Doomed for Failure." *San Antonio Light,* (October 18, 1988).

16. Joseph A. Fernandez quoted in *The New York Times* (July 27, 1988).

17. Criteria to evaluate School-Based Management Application: Memorandum jointly issued by Joseph A. Fernandez and Pat L. Turnillo, "Request for Proposals to Participate in School Based Management/Shared Decision-Making (SBM/SDM) Pilot Group Program II." Attachment B, "Proposal Assessment Criteria." (October 12, 1988).

18. L. Gold, "Pennsylvania District Will Test 'Shared Governance.' " *Education Week* (June 8, 1988).

19. "School-Based Management: The Door to Improvement?" *ASCD Update.* vol. 31, no. 1 (1989), p. 1.

20. "Teacher Involvement in Decisionmaking: A State-by-State Profile." Carnegie Foundation for the Advancement of Teaching (Princeton, N.J.: 1987).

21. Arnold Tannenbaum: *Control in Organization* (New York: McGraw Hill, 1968).

22. Lynne Miller, "Unlikely Beginnings: The District Office as a Starting Point for Developing a Professional Culture for Teaching." *Building a Professional Culture in Schools.* Ann Lieberman, ed. (New York: Teachers College Press, 1988), pp. 185–222.

23. Lynn Olsen, "In San Diego, Managers Forging 'Service' Role." *Education Week,* March 8, 1989, p. 8.

24. Henry M. Levin, "Structuring Schools for Greater Effectiveness with Educationally Disadvantaged or At-Risk Children." Paper presented to the American Educational Research Association, (New Orleans, April 7, 1988).

25. Cecilia Estrada. Remarks prepared for the Holmes group seminar on "Equity, Diversity, and the Organization of Schools," Michigan State University. Sept. 25–26, 1988.

26. "The Sherman School Story An Interview with Dennis Doyle." *Democratic Schools* (Summer, 1988) p. 10.

27. "Schools Can't Do it Alone," *Principal's Exchange,* Westchester Principals' Center. vol. 4, no. 2, Spring 1989. p. 2.

28. Deborah L. Cohen. "Growing Number of Schools Are Filling Demand for Child Care." *Education Week,* April 19, 1989.

29. Rosabeth MossKanter, *Men and Women of the Corporation* (New York: Basic Books, 1977), pp. 246–248.

Chapter 9

1. Susan J. Rosenholtz, *Teacher's Workplace: A Social-organizational Analysis* (New York: Longman, 1989).

2. Judith Warren Little, *School Success and Staff Development in Urban Desegregated Schools: A Summary of Recently Completed Research* Boulder, Colorado: Center for Action Research, 1981).

3. Henry Mintzberg, *The Structuring of Organizations* (Englewood Cliffs, NJ: Prentice Hall, Inc. 1979)

4. Rosabeth Moss Kanter, *Men and Women of the Corporation* (New York: Basic Books, 1977).

5. Mibrey Wallin McLaughlin and Sylvia Mei-Ling Yee. "School as a Place to Have a Career." *Building a Professional Culture in Schools.* Ann Lieberman, ed., (New York: Teachers College Press, 1988).

6. *Ibid.,* p. 35.

7. Robert H. Hayes, "Strategic Planning—Forward in Reverse?" *Harvard Business Review.* (Nov–Dec. 1985), p. 114.

8. Alan Smith, presentation to the University Club of Chicago, Ill. (December 6, 1988).

9. Robert J. Sternberg, *The Triarchic Mind: A New Theory of Human Intelligence* (New York: Viking Press, 1988), p. 297.

10. *Ibid.* p. 279.

11. Edward L. Deci and Richard M. Ryan, *Intrinsic Motivation and Self-Determination in Human Behavior* (New York: Plenum Press, 1985).

12. *Ibid.*

13. Frederick Herzberg, *Work and the Nature of Man* (New York: World Publishing Co., 1966).

14. J. R. Hackman and Greg Oldman, "Motivation Through the Design of Work." *Organizational Behavior and Human Performance.* vol. 16, no. 2 (1976).

15. Mihaly Csikszentmihalyi, *Beyond Boredom and Anxiety* (San Francisco: Jossey-Bass, 1975).

16. In addition to Deci and Ryan: Herzberg; Csikszentmihalyi; and Hackman and Oldman cited above see Robert W. White, "Motivation Reconsidered: The Concept of Competence." *Psychological Review.* vol. 66, no. 5 (1959) and Richard De Charms, *Personal Causation* (New York: Academic Press, 1968).

17. Patricia T. Ashton and Rodman B. Webb, *Making a Difference: Teachers Sense of Efficacy and Student Achievement* (New York: Longman, 1986).

18. Thomas J. Sergiovanni and Robert J. Starratt. *Supervision: Human Perspectives* (New York: McGraw Hill, 1988). p. 135.

Chapter 10

1. Nathan Mathis, "Houston Chief Pursues 'Tough Policy.' " *Education Week*, (June 15, 1988), p. 4.

2. William Snider, "Houston School Chief's 'Get Tough' Policy Will Send 40,000 to After-School Tutorials." *Education Week* (Feb. 17, 1988), p. 25.

3. "At Wilson It's a Whole New Ball Game." *Business Week* June 6, 1988.

4. Texas Commissioner of Education William Kirby quoted in the *San Antonio Light* (Nov. 11, 1988), p. A–12.

5. Texas Commissioner of Education William Kirby quoted in the *San Antonio Light* (Nov. 22, 1988), p. A–8.

6. Peter Vaill, "The Purposing of High Performing Systems" *Leadership and Organizational Culture.* T. J. Sergiovanni and J. E. Corbally, eds., (Urbana: University of Illinois Press, 1984). p. 103.

7. "How Schools Change: Bat and Bull Horn on Democratic Control." *Democratic Schools.* (Summer 1988), p. 3.

8. "The Sherman School Story: An Interview with Dennis Doyle." *Democratic Schools,* (Summer, 1988) pp. 6–7.

9. Council of Chief State School Officers, "Elements of a Model State Statute." *School Success for Students at Risk* (Orlando: Harcourt Brace Jovanovich, 1988), pp. 320–346.

10. David W. Hornbeck, "All our children." *Ibid.,* p. 8.

11. This discussion of resilient and flexible leadership follows closely that which appears in T. J. Sergiovanni, *The Principalship A Reflective Practice Perspective* (Boston: Allyn and Bacon, 1987). pp. 88–92.

12. William J. Reddin, *Managerial Effectiveness* (New York: McGraw-Hill, 1970), pp. 258, 259, 266, 271.

13. Immanuel Kant, "Theory into Practice." *Kant's Political Writings.* Translated by Hans Reiss (Cambridge 1970), p. 74.

Chapter 11

1. David T. Kearns and Denis P. Doyle, *Winning the Brain Race A Bold Plan to Make Our Schools Competitive.* (San Francisco: Institute for Contemporary Studies, 1988.) p. 52.

2. Keith Goldhammer, Gerald Becker, Richard Withycombe, Frank Doyel, Edgar Miller, Claude Morgan, Louis De Loretto and Bill Aldridge, *Elementary School Principals and Their Schools.* (Eugene: University of Oregon Center for the Advanced Study of Educational Administration, 1971.) p. 2.

3. Peter Block believes that choices: Peter Block, *The Empowered Manager* (San Francisco: Jossey-Bass, 1987.) p. 11.

4. *Ibid.,* p. 16.

5. Lynn Olsen, "A Seattle Principle Defies the Conventional Wisdom." *Education Week.* April 13, 1988. pp. 1–5.

6. *Ibid.,* p.

7. Alan L. Wilkins. *Developing Corporate Character.* (San Francisco: Jossey-Bass, 1989.) p. 37.

8. *Ibid.*, p. 27.

9. Terrence E. Deal, "Cultural Change: Opportunity, Silent Killer, or Metamorphosis" in R. H. Killman, M. J. Saxton, R. Serpt and Associates, *Gaining Control of the Corporate Culture.* (San Francisco: Jossey-Bass, 1985.)

10. Wilkins, *op.cit.*, pp. 52–60.

11. Deal, *op.cit.*, 1985.

12. Ruby Cremaschi-Schwimmer, remarks prepared for the Holmes Group Seminar on Tomorrow's Schools. Michigan State University, Dec. 9, 1988.

13. Robert K. Greenleaf, *Servant Leadership.* (New York: Paulist Press, 1977.) p. 29 as quoted in Arthur Blumberg, "Some Not Quite Random Thoughts About Leadership." *Wingspan.* Vol. 4, No. 1, 1988. p. 5.

14. The Steve Johnson story including quotes is from Ginger Hall, "Principal Tames Tough Schools; in Running for $1 million Grant." *San Antonio Express-News.* Jan. 3, 1989, p. 8A.

15. Roland S. Barth, "School: A Community of Leaders." in Ann Lieberman (editor). *Building a Professional Culture in Schools.* (New York: Teachers' College Press, 1988.) p. 146.

16. Robert E. Kelley, "In Praise of Followers." *Harvard Business Review.* Nov.–Dec., 1988, p. 144.

17. *Ibid.*

18. Robert S. Gilchrist, *Effective Schools: Three Case Studies of Excellence.* (Bloomington, Ind.: National Educational Service, 1989.) p. 85.

Index

A 9
B 0
C 1
D 2
E 3
F 4
G 5
H 6
I 7
J 8